Theosophy in the Qabbālāh

A Sunrise Library Book

THEOSOPHY
in the
QABBĀLĀH

Grace F. Knoche

THEOSOPHICAL UNIVERSITY PRESS
PASADENA, CALIFORNIA

THEOSOPHICAL UNIVERSITY PRESS
POST OFFICE BOX C
PASADENA, CALIFORNIA 91109-7107
www.theosociety.org
2006

Copyright © 2006 by Theosophical University Press

Library of Congress Cataloging-in-Publication Data

Knoche, Grace F.
    Theosophy in the Qabbālāh / Grace F. Knoche.
        p. cm.
    Includes bibliographical references and index.
        ISBN-13: 978-1-55700-183-2 (hardcover : alk. paper)
        ISBN-10: 1-55700-183-9 (hardcover : alk. paper)
        ISBN-13: 978-1-55700-184-9 (pbk. : alk. paper)
        ISBN-10: 1-55700-184-7 (pbk. : alk. paper)
    1. Cabala—History. 2. Sefirot (Cabala)
    3. Zohar. 4. Theosophy. I. Title.
BM526.K66 2006
296.1′6—dc22
                                    2006014145

Manufactured in the United States of America

Contents

And they that be wise shall shine as the brightness
of the firmament . . .　　　　— *Daniel* 12:3

Foreword

THIS BOOK ORIGINATED IN a lecture series given in the 1940s at Theosophical University, Point Loma, California, and also in the San Diego area. Its objective is to distill from the vast range of Qabbalistic literature those essentials which bear the stamp of the archaic tradition; in other words, a presentation in broad outline of the theosophy in the Qabbālāh. Obviously the present study does not comprise all that Qabbālāh teaches, nor is any theme handled exhaustively. It is hoped that the esotericism of the original Chaldean Qabbālāh (the occult basis of the Hebrew Qabbālāh) will be recognized for what it is: one of the theosophies of antiquity, inherited by the Hebrews from the ancient Chaldeans, who received this "theosophy of the angels" from the Council of the Wise.

Transliteration and pronunciation of Hebrew are discussed in Appendix 1. Transliteration of Hebrew and Aramaic terms is based on the system used by G. de Purucker of Theosophical University, updated through consultation with current systems. Appendix 2 is a glossary of the Qabbalistic terms included in this study, with their derivation, as this often yields insight into a term's philosophic connotation and its relationship with other terms.

— G. F. K.

The Theosophical Society
Pasadena, California, USA
February 15, 2006

Theosophy in the Qabbālāh

1

Introduction to Qabbalistic Literature

QABBĀLĀH IS NOT A BOOK OR BOOKS. It is an ancient mystical tradition. H. P. Blavatsky (HPB) comments:

> Kabalah is no special volume, nor is it even a system. It consists of seven different systems applied to seven different interpretations of any given Esoteric work or subject. These systems were always *transmitted orally* by one generation of Initiates to another, under the pledge of the Sodalian oath, and *they have never been recorded in writing* by any one. . . . It is not allied to "tradition" but to the seven veils or the seven truths orally *revealed at Initiation*. . . . Thus, if Kabalah as a word is Hebrew, the system itself is no more Jewish than is sunlight; it is universal.
>
> — *H. P. Blavatsky: Collected Writings* 7:268

The word *qabbālāh* means "to receive, to admit a precept," hence admission or reception by heart and mind of esoteric knowledge. It is secret wisdom not sought by the many, but revealed "only in darkness and with mouth to ear." Thus, the Tōrāh or Pentateuch is called the Law; the Talmūd, the soul of the Law; and Qabbālāh, the soul of the soul of the Law.

Qabbālāh is the stream of esoteric wisdom, and only the initiated were entrusted with its *Sōd* or Mysteries. Legend has it that its secret wisdom is traceable back to the Deity, who communicated the doctrine to a "select company of angels." These formed a "theosophic school in Paradise," where Qabbālāh was taught to them in order that, after the fall, they might teach Adam and Eve (early humanity), thus enabling mankind to exercise free will and acquire self-conscious nobility and wisdom. But *nothing esoteric was ever written down*: it was considered a desecration to commit esoteric truth to writing, for the written word cannot contain the inner truth, being but a symbol, the rind or bark. The secret wisdom was held to be incommunicable except by master to pupil.

The Jews have preserved among their mystical works two important books on Qabbālāh. The first, *Sēfer Yĕtsīrāh*, "The Book of Formation (or Creation)," treats of cosmogony in particular, i.e., the genesis of worlds through numbers and letters. The interrelations of the 22 letters of the Hebrew alphabet with the 10 numbers form the 32 marvelous paths of wisdom. The human being is regarded as the synthesis of the 22 letters which, with the addition of the ten sĕfīrōth or "numbers," make the complete synthesis of creation. Just as alphabetic characters form the structure of speech and its communication of intelligence, so the characters of the Hebrew alphabet symbolize the elements of the universe: in, above, and around the elements of the universe there is the divine hierarchy, of which the elements are the outward expressions. The 22 letters are sometimes divided into Three Mothers — a triad, a heptad, and a dodecad — corresponding to the three primal letters A M S (ס מ א), the seven planets, and the twelve signs of the zodiac. The author of *Sēfer Yĕtsīrāh* is not known. It was formerly attributed to the patriarch Abraham, but is generally reputed to be by Rabbi 'Aqībā', the teacher of Rabbi Shim'ōn ben Yoḥai.

The second and best known book on Qabbālāh is *Sēfer-hā-Zohar*, the "Book of Brightness, Splendor, or Light." The bulk of the Zoharic writings, outside of commentary on the Pentateuch itself, comprises eleven treatises.* Three principal books of the *Zohar* are *Hā-'Idrā' Rabbā' Qaddīshā'* (The Great Holy Assembly), *Hā-'Idrā' Zūṭā' Qaddīshā'* (The Small Holy Assembly), and *Sifrā' di-Tsĕnī'ūthā'* (Book of Concealment).† Of this last and its relation to the Stanzas of Dzyan, upon which *The Secret Doctrine* is based, HPB writes:

> There exists somewhere in this wide world an old Book — so very old that our modern antiquarians might ponder over its pages an indefinite time, and still not quite agree as to the nature of the fabric upon which it is written. It is the only original copy now in existence. The most ancient Hebrew document on occult learning — the *Siphra Dzeniouta* — was compiled from it, and that at a time when the former was already considered in the light of a literary relic. — *Isis Unveiled* 1:1

This viewpoint is not accepted by the majority of scholars. Gershom G. Scholem, for example, held the reverse: that the Stanzas of Dzyan were derived from the *Sifrā' di-*

---

*See Appendix, "Zoharic Writings."

†Translated into English from the Latin rendition of Knorr von Rosenroth by S. Liddell MacGregor Mathers.

Tsĕnī'ūthā'. Whatever the case, there is a striking similarity between the *Zohar* and the Stanzas of Dzyan insofar as they relate to the emanation or coming forth of worlds from the Boundless.

In the thirteenth century the *Zohar* was published by Rabbi Moses de Leon of Guadalajara, Spain, and he attributed it to Rabbi Shim'ōn ben Yoḥai. That Moses de Leon is the author or editor of the *Zohar* is most likely.* That he had recourse to ancient manuscripts dating from the days of Shim'ōn ben Yoḥai is almost certain.

On this point HPB says:

> The author [Isaac Myer] of the "Qabbalah" makes several attempts to prove conclusively the antiquity of the Zohar. Thus he shows that Moses de Leon could not be the author or the forger of the Zoharic works in the XIIIth century, as he is accused of being, since Ibn Gebirol gave out the same philosophical teaching 225 years before the day of Moses de Leon. No true Kabalist or scholar will ever deny the fact. It is certain that Ibn Gebirol based his doctrines upon the oldest Kabalistic sources, namely, the "Chaldean Book of Numbers," as well as some no longer extant Midrashim, the same, no doubt, as those used by Moses de Leon. But it is just the difference between the two ways of treating the same esoteric subjects, which, while proving the enormous antiquity of the esoteric system, points to a decided ring of Talmudistic and even Christian sectarianism in the compilation and glossaries of the Zoharic system by Rabbi Moses. Ibn Gebirol *never quoted from the Scriptures* to enforce the teachings. Moses de Leon has made of the *Zohar*

---

*Cf. *Major Trends in Jewish Mysticism*, pp. 153-201.

that which it has remained to this day, "a running commentary on the . . . Books of the Pentateuch," with a few later additions made by Christian hands. One follows the archaic esoteric philosophy; the other, only that portion which was adapted to the *lost* Books of Moses restored by Ezra. Thus, while the system, or the trunk on which the primitive original *Zohar* was engrafted, is of an immense antiquity many of the (later) Zoharic offshoots are strongly coloured by the peculiar views held by Christian Gnostics (Syrian and Chaldean), the friends and co-workers of Moses de Leon who, as shown by Munk, accepted their interpretations.

— *The Secret Doctrine* 2:461n

This production appeared at the end of the thirteenth century, a century noted for its brilliant spiritual and intellectual lights. It created a sensation and ushered in what is known as the period of Spanish Qabbalism. Here we have two centuries of splendor in Spain, when the Moors likewise were in full flower.

It was not until the middle and last quarter of the fifteenth century that a number of significant events occurred: the expulsion of the Jews from Spain in 1492 under Ferdinand and Isabella; the shipping trade with India had begun; the Reformation of Luther was soon to occur; and, also in 1492, the New World opened up. During this period and following two centuries the Gentiles — through Pico della Mirándola, Cardinal Nicolao Cusani, John Trithemius, Henry Cornelius Agrippa, Paracelsus, the Van Helmonts, John Reuchlin, Henry Khunrath, Jerome Cardan, Guillaume Postel, Christian Knorr (Baron) von Rosenroth, Athanasius Kircher, and, not least, Jacob Boehme — became captivated with the Qabbalistic interpretation of Christianity. This had a far-reaching influence on the whole of Europe, liberating spiritual thinking as well as higher learning. Several English mystics show the influence of Qabbalistic thought, such as Henry More, Philip Bailey, John Colet, Robert Fludd, Raymond Lully, Thomas Vaughan (Eugenius Philalethes), and the poet Thomas Traherne. Isaac Myer points to Qabbalistic influence on European literature:

> Upon the Practical Qabbalah, Abbe de Villars (nephew of De Montfaucon) in 1670, published his celebrated satirical novel, The Count de Gabalis, upon which Pope based his Rape of the Lock. Qabbalism runs through the Medieval poem, the Romance of the Rose, and permeates the writings of Dante. — *Qabbalah*, p. 171

It is not our intent to trace the spiritual and intellectual expansion that began during the middle of the fifteenth century. Suffice to note that Qabbalistic thought had a continuing and lasting influence upon such thinkers as Spinoza, Leibniz, Newton, Kepler, and Francis Bacon.

Today we can find expressions of the original esoteric Qabbalistic knowledge in modern theosophical works. We now turn our attention to a consideration of some of the basic concepts of Qabbalistic philosophy.

2

How the One Becomes the Many

QABBĀLĀH DEALS IN LARGE PART with the doctrine of emanation. It describes in pictorial fashion a tree of life ('*ēts ḥayyīm*) formed of ten emanations or *sĕfīrōth* issuing forth from the Boundless ('*ein sōf*). Sĕfīrāh means "number" or "emanation"—the concept of the universe being established in and on numbers is found also in the doctrines of Pythagoras, while the image of a cosmic tree is common to many cultures.

The Sĕfīrōthal Tree is a symbol of man, atom, star, or any other hierarchy. It depicts the Qabbalistic method of describing the series of emanations that the One or divine monad of any being unfolds from within itself in assuming full imbodiment. The sĕfīrōth represent the Jewish way of describing the various aspects of universal manifestation.

'*Ein sōf* (without boundary or limit) is equivalent to the Sanskrit *parabrahman* (beyond Brahman). From it issue at karmic intervals universes great and small. The Boundless itself has no attributes, but so subtle was the Qabbalistic mind that it conceived the Boundless as containing a series of "concealed sĕfīrōth." While completely unmanifest, these nevertheless exhibit *in potentia* a three-in-one or a

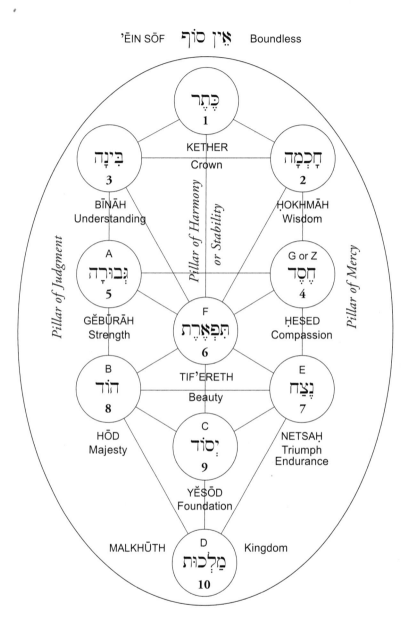

'ĒIN SŌF אֵין סוֹף Boundless

כֶּתֶר
1
KETHER
Crown

בִּינָה
3
BĪNĀH
Understanding

חָכְמָה
2
HOKHMĀH
Wisdom

Pillar of Harmony or Stability

Pillar of Judgment

Pillar of Mercy

A
גְּבוּרָה
5
GĔBŪRĀH
Strength

G or Z
חֶסֶד
4
ḤESED
Compassion

F
תִּפְאֶרֶת
6
TIF'ERETH
Beauty

B
הוֹד
8
HŌD
Majesty

E
נֶצַח
7
NETSAḤ
Triumph
Endurance

C
יְסוֹד
9
YĔSŌD
Foundation

MALKHŪTH
D
מַלְכוּת
10
Kingdom

The Sĕfīrōthal Tree

one-in-three garment of nonbeing: *'ayin,* "no-thing-ness," the darkness of pure nonbeing, which produced *'ēin sōf,* "boundless" expanse of space; and the union of these two brought forth *'ēin sōf 'ōr,* "boundless or limitless light," the primal light of pre-manifestation.*

When the Boundless or *'ēin sōf* wished to exhibit an aspect of itself, this three-in-one veil of nonbeing contracted or, as the *Zohar* phrases it, "concentrated its essence" into a single point: the boundless expanse condensed into the one primordial point (*nĕqūdāh ri'shōnāh,* also called *nĕqūdāh qadmā'āh*), which point they called Sĕfīrāh, primal number or emanation. Having thus "concentrated" its divine essence in Sĕfīrāh, it again expanded and a universe of tenfold character unfolded into manifestation. This process of contraction and expansion is called *tsimtsūm* (tension) and the resulting "expanded or smooth point" is called *nĕqūdāh pĕshūṭāh.* The universe so produced is the sĕfīrōthal tree of life. From Sĕfīrāh, called likewise Kether the Crown, issued forth in time and space nine lower sĕfīrōth or emanations of graduated spiritual and material texture.

This emanational procession is described again and again in the *Zohar,* as in the following passages:

> When the Hidden of all the Hidden, willed to manifest Itself, It first made a point (Kether, the first Sephirah . . .), shaped it into a Sacred Form (*i.e.,* the totality of all the Sephiroth, the Adam Illa-ah, or Adam Qadmon) and covered it with a rich and splendid garment, that is the universe.
>
> — *Zohar* 1:2a, Myer, *Qabbalah,* pp. 280-81

---

*See Mathers, *Kabbalah,* pp. 20-1 and diagram.

The Aged of the Aged, the Unknown of the Unknown, has a form, and yet no form. He has a form whereby the universe is preserved, and yet has no form, because he cannot be comprehended. When he first assumed a form (in Sephirah, his first emanation), he caused nine splendid lights to emanate from it. — *Zohar* 3:288a, quoted in *Isis Unveiled* 2:214

Various are the ways in which the Boundless is portrayed as emanating a succession of sĕfīrōthal trees: at one time the sĕfīrōth are described as sparks from the central fire; also as ten vessels into which the life-stream from 'ēin sōf flows; and still again as a series of concentric spheres. They all attempt to describe the indescribable: the issuing forth of finite entities from "the infinite bosom of Duration," to quote from the "Book of Dzyan." From this archaic manuscript H. P. Blavatsky used seven stanzas as the foundation of her masterwork, *The Secret Doctrine*.

It is intriguing to observe the close similarity of fundamental tenet between the Stanzas of Dzyan and the doctrine of emanation found in Qabbālāh. HPB states that these stanzas

give an abstract formula which can be applied, *mutatis mutandis*, to all evolution: to that of our tiny earth, to that of the chain of planets of which that earth forms one, to the solar Universe to which that chain belongs, and so on, in an ascending scale, till the mind reels and is exhausted in the effort. — *SD* 1:20-1

The same may be said of the fundamental doctrines of Qabbālāh: they can be applied analogically to the evolution of man, planet, solar system, or galaxy.

To quote now a few ślokas from the Stanzas of Dzyan as an aid to understanding the Zohar:

Darkness alone filled the boundless all, for father, mother and son were once more one, and the son had not awakened yet for the new wheel, and his pilgrimage thereon (1:5).

Alone the one form of existence stretched boundless, infinite, causeless, in dreamless sleep; and life pulsated unconscious in universal space, throughout that all-presence which is sensed by the opened eye of the Dangma (1:8).

The hour had not yet struck; the ray had not yet flashed into the Germ; the Matripadma [Mother-lotus] had not yet swollen (2:3).

The last vibration of the seventh eternity thrills through infinitude. The mother swells, expanding from within without, like the bud of the lotus (3:1).

The vibration sweeps along, touching with its swift wing the whole universe and the germ that dwelleth in darkness: the darkness that breathes over the slumbering waters of life (3:2).

Darkness radiates light, and light drops one solitary ray into the mother-deep. The ray shoots through the virgin egg; the ray causes the eternal egg to thrill, and drop the non-eternal germ, which condenses into the world-egg (3:3).

Behold, oh Lanoo! The radiant child of the two, the unparalleled refulgent glory: Bright Space Son of Dark Space, which emerges from the depths of the great dark waters (3:7).

Where was the germ and where was now darkness? Where is the spirit of the flame that burns in thy lamp, oh Lanoo? (3:8)

It expands when the breath of fire is upon it; it contracts when the breath of the mother touches it. Then the sons dissociate and scatter, to return into their mother's bosom at the end of the great day, and re-become one with her; when it is cooling it becomes radiant, and the sons expand and contract through their own selves and hearts; they embrace infinitude (3:11).   — *SD* 1:27-30

Turning to Qabbālāh we discover the same ideas. "Darkness alone filled the Boundless All" recalls *'ayin*, "no-thing," filling all the spaces of space — that condition of no-thing-ness where the seeds of future sĕfīrōthal trees of cosmic lives are still sleeping in darkness. From *'ayin*, darkness or no-thing-ness, comes *'ēin sōf*, limitless or boundless fields of infinitude: the "one form of existence" that stretches "boundless, infinite, causeless, in dreamless sleep." 'Ēin sōf, the mystery of mysteries, is called in the *Zohar* the "closed eye" because the lives sleeping therein do not perceive what is "sensed by the opened eye of the Dangma [initiate]," which "opened eye" in Qabbālāh is termed Kether, the Crown or first emanation. As the *Zohar* states:

> When the Unknown of the Unknown wished to manifest Itself, It began by producing a point; as long as that luminous point had not gone out of Its bosom, the Infinite was still completely unknown and diffused no light.
>
> — 1:2a, Myer, p. 127

The luminous or light point, however, does periodically "appear through its energy," for the seeds of future worlds cannot remain forever within the closed eye of 'ēin sōf. The vibration of the incoming universe or sĕfīrōthal tree quickens the sleeping seeds, and the "Light that was wrapped in Darkness," as the *Zohar* phrases it, floods the expanse. 'Ēin sōf has become 'ēin sōf 'ōr: infinite space has become infinite light. "Bright Space Son of Dark Space" as the Stanzas of Dzyan express it: the primordial quiver of manifestation, which is the source and forerunner of later multiplication and consequent division of the One into the many. We may here conceive of darkness as pure spirit, and light as matter.

"The ray shoots through the virgin egg" — precisely the bursting forth of that "luminous point" of Qabbālāh into Kether, and from Kether, the first Sĕfīrāh, into the nine inferior lights, until a complete tenfold sĕfīrōthal tree of lives is unfolded.

"It expands when the breath of fire is upon it; it contracts when the breath of the mother touches it" is a precise description of tsimtsūm. Qabbālāh states that when the Divine, the Holy, wishes to send forth or emanate a ray from itself through the "closed eye" of 'ēin sōf into the "eye, opened" of Kether, by a mysterious process of will (*rātsōn*) it "concentrated its essence" into a single point, and this concentration of power and energy is called tsimtsūm, signifying the "contraction" and subsequent expansion characteristic of manifestation.

Through tsimtsūm, the primordial point expanded, and a second point ("smooth or expanded point") was produced, which in turn by a continuing process of tsimtsūm brought forth the succeeding sĕfīrōth. As the *Zohar* describes it, the primordial point

was an inner light which had no limit so that could be known, its pureness, thinness (subtility) and clearness, until it expanded itself through itself; and the expansion of this point made a palace to envelope that point. Its (the palace's) light cannot be comprehended because of its immense pureness and yet it is not so thin (subtile) and clear as that first point, which is hidden and concealed. The palace which is the garment to that hidden point, its light (is also) unlimited, although it is not so pure and clear as that first point which is hidden and concealed. That palace expands itself outwardly from its first light, and that expansion is the garment to that palace, of which its inner is subtile and clear; and from here, (each) farther spreads itself one in another, and envelopes itself, one in another, until it is found, (that) one is a garment to the other, and the other still to another; . . .   — 1:20b, Myer, p. 381

This primordial point — *nĕqūdāh qadmā'āh*, otherwise Kether, the first sĕfīrāh — expands and makes "a palace," i.e., produces from within itself the next sĕfīrāh; that second sĕfīrāh, while a "palace" or "envelope" or garment to the first sĕfīrāh, itself becomes the "inner light" to the succeeding sĕfīrāh; which in its turn is both "palace" to the second sĕfīrāh and "inner light" to the fourth sĕfīrāh; and so the process continues throughout the tenfold tree. The same takes place with the four Adams (see ch. 7), where each succeeding Adam functions both as prototype to the one below, and reflection of the one above; at one time transmitter of the light, at another a receiver.

In the *Zohar* the "inner light" is called *būtsīnā'*, a word meaning "light" or "candle," frequently found in the phrase *Būtsīnā' dĕQardīnūtha'*, translated by Myer (p. 381) as "the brilliant inner Light" which "came out from the Hidden of

Hidden, from the Head of the Ain Soph" (1:3). Or again, the *Zohar* has:

> Come, See! At the time it came up in the Will of the Holy, Blessed be He! to create the world, He brought forth from the *Botzeen-ah Qardinuthah* [*Būtsīnā' děQardīnūthā'*], *i.e.*, the very inner light (of the heart) a knot (or, chain) and lighted (emanated) the darkness from it and let it down Below. The darkness lighted in a hundred different ways and paths, small and great, and made the House (Tabernacle or Temple, Below. Rev. xi, 19; xv, 5, 6, 8; xvi, 1.) of the world. — 1:172a, Myer, p. 385

Several additional names are used by the Qabbalists for both Kether and 'ēin sōf. No term was ever satisfactory, for how could the finite mind, no matter how reverent or disciplined in esoteric thought, ever describe that which has neither attribute, form, nor color? They compromised, therefore, by giving 'ēin sōf various suggestive titles, each an attempt to portray an aspect of the infinite. These titles, however, were quite as often used to describe the first manifestation from 'ēin sōf — Kether, the Holy Ancient — as a seed or point. Careful study of the context usually enables one to detect to which of the two these terms apply.

Some of the titles given in the *Zohar* to 'ēin sōf, and often to Kether, are: the Ancient of the Ancient Ones (*'attīqā' dě'attīqīn*); Ancient of all the Ancient Ones (*'attīqā' dě-kol 'attīqīn*); Hidden of the Hidden Ones (*těmīrā' ditěmīrīn*); Concealed of the Concealed Ones (*sithrā' děsithrīn*); Oldest of the Oldest (*sābā' děsābīn*); Archaic Oldest of the Oldest, or Eternal Ancient of the Ancients (*'attīqā' sābā' děsābīn*);

Holy Ancient One (*'attīqā' qaddīshā'*); and Unknown of all the Unknown Ones or Hidden of all the Hidden Ones (*sĕthīmā' dĕ-kol sĕthīmīn*).

All of these titles selected from different books of the *Zohar* revolve around one thought: the utterly unknowable and hid character of the Boundless. As the *Zohar* (2:42-3) says: "This first Sefirah is sometimes called the Infinite (Ayn Sof), sometimes the Supreme Crown (Kether Elyon), and sometimes the No-Thing (Ay-yin) or the Place (Mokom) [*māqōm*]. . . . we must take care not to confound it ['Ayin] with the Ancient of Ancients ['attīqā' dĕ'attīqīn], that is to say, with the Ayn-Sof Himself, before whom the most dazzling light is but a shadow."*

How does the Qabbalistic description of the coming into being of the universe harmonize with that of *Genesis* in the Tōrāh? The standard English translations are deceptive. For example, the first word in the Bible is *rē'shīth* — "beginning, headship," "the most excellent or highest of a series," "wisdom" — prefixed by the preposition *bĕ*, meaning "in, through," or "by means of." The beginning of *Genesis*, then, may quite correctly be translated "by wisdom," or "by means of wisdom," or "by or in a multitude," as G. de Purucker does in *Fundamentals of the Esoteric Philosophy* (2nd ed., pp. 98-102). HPB maintains that:

> Origen, Clemens Alexandrinus, Chalcidius, Methodius, and Maimonides, on the authority of the *Targum* of Jerusalem, the orthodox and greatest authority of the Jews, held

---

*Franck, *Kabbalah*, p. 99n33 and pp. 158-9; cf. also Mathers, *Idrā' Rabbā'*, pp. 21, 23; and Ginsburg, p. 89.

that the first two words in the book of *Genesis* — B-RASIT [bĕrē'shīth], mean *Wisdom*, or the *Principle*. And that the idea of these words meaning "*in the beginning*" was never shared but by the profane, who were not allowed to penetrate any deeper into the esoteric sense of the sentence.

— *Isis Unveiled* 2:35

The fathers . . . dreaded above all to have the esoteric and true meaning of the word *Rasit* [rē'shīth] unveiled to the multitudes; for if once the true sense of this sentence, as well as that of the Hebrew word *asdt*. . . were understood rightly, the mystery of the Christian trinity would have crumbled, carrying in its downfall the new religion into the same heap of ruins with the ancient Mysteries.   — Ibid. 2:34

In his *Fundamentals* (p. 99), Purucker translates the word *'elohīm* in the first verse of *Genesis* as plural: "in a host (or multitude) the gods ['*elohīm*] formed (made) themselves into the heavens and the earth." *Genesis* 1:2 is usually translated "And the earth was without form, and void." The two words (*tohū* and *bohū*) for the primeval chaos preceding the appearance of the manifestation, are similar in meaning. *Tohū* signifies that which lies waste, without inhabitants or other manifested activity; and *bohū* signifies empty or void. Thus together they mean "uninhabited void," which corresponds to the Greek Χάος (chaos), the homogeneous condition of our solar system or galaxy before manifestation began. Purucker's literal translation of the first verses of *Genesis* continues:

"And darkness upon the face of the ethers. And the rūahh (the spirit-soul) of the gods (of Elohīm) (fluttered, hovered) brooding.". . .

And said (the) Elohīm (the gods) — light, come-into-being! and light came-into-being. And saw (the) gods the light, that (it was) good. And divided Elohīm between the light and between the darkness. And called Elohīm the light day, and the darkness called they night. And (there) came-into-being eve, and (there) came-into-being morn. Day one. — *Fundamentals*, p. 100

3

The Sĕfīrōthal Tree

THE FIRST AND FOREMOST "emanation" from 'ēin sōf, the
Boundless, is the first of the sĕfīrōth, called Sĕfīrāh (see diagram p. 10). It is the primordial point from which emanate
nine lower sĕfīrōth in serial order and in descending quality
of brightness. This first sĕfīrāh is commonly called *Kether*
(diadem, crown), and is known by various other names,
such as White Head, Ancient of Days, Macroprosopus or
Great Face — called Great Face because it contains poten-
tially all the other "small" faces or lower sĕfīrōth. The term
face is used to signify the ancient idea of the mask or *māyā*,
and Great Face signifies the cosmic illusion of manifestation, called in Sanskrit *mahā-māyā*.

Kether is Number One, Indivisible, the monad of Pythagoras, the *Monas monadum* of Leibniz. From one standpoint it is the first unmanifest Logos. Its divine name is
'ehyeh ("I am"). In one system of correspondences, Kether
is made equivalent to the *Primum Mobile*, the first cosmic
spatial manifestation of divinity; in another to the central
invisible sun. When correlated to 'Ādām Qadmōn (archetypal man or universe), Kether is the head or "crown" of
the head.

From Kether (crown), the indivisible point, issue forth

two rays of active and passive — or masculine and feminine — potency.* The right and masculine energy is focused in Ḥokhmāh (wisdom), the second sĕfīrāh, termed the Duad, 'āb (father), likewise called by its divine name, yāh. It corresponds in certain respects to the second Logos, and represents the right shoulder of 'Ādām Qadmōn. The third sĕfīrāh, Bīnāh (intelligence, insight, understanding), is the feminine passive stream of energy flowing from Kether through Ḥokhmāh, and forms the left shoulder of 'Ādām Qadmōn. Its divine name is heh. It is also called 'ēm or 'immī (the Mother), coequal with the Father. Bīnāh is the Supernal Mother as contrasted with the tenth sĕfīrāh, Malkhūth, the inferior Mother, Bride, or Queen. Bīnāh is the third Logos from one viewpoint.

These three sĕfīrōth form the invisible triad of archetypal man. As Qabbalistic thought expresses it: "neither the Head nor the shoulders of Adam-Kadmon can be seen" (cf. SD 1:239). The position of Ḥokhmāh and Bīnāh as the second and third — respectively the masculine or Father, and the feminine or Mother — is by certain Qabbalists reversed, Isaac Myer among these (Qabbalah, pp. 259-60). There is much to be said in favor of the reverse position, with Bīnāh as the feminine aspect representing the Mother issuing first from Kether, the two giving birth to or emanating Ḥokhmāh as the Son. This placing would immediately identify these first three sĕfīrōth, or the first "face" of the Tree of Life, with the Hindu Trimūrti of Brahmā,

---

*Each sĕfīrāh is feminine or receptive to the one above, and masculine or transmitting to the one below it; cf. Mathers, pp. 27, 335nn.

Vishnu, and Śiva, and with the Christian Trinity as originally understood as Father, Holy Spirit, and Son. However, as many students of Qabbālāh leave this refinement of position alone and take the more general view of Ḥokhmāh and Bīnāh as being the second and third aspects respectively, we shall place them likewise. It is of small moment which one of them is placed second or third, the essential point being that the supernal triad of Kether, Ḥokhmāh, and Bīnāh represents the unmanifest triad of divine forces and powers, which in time and space emanate from themselves the remaining sĕfīrōthal powers in orderly progression.

As a direct emanation from this triad, the second "face" or triad is born, consisting of Ḥesed, Gĕbūrāh, and Tif'-ereth: Compassion, Strength, and Beauty. *Ḥesed* (ardor, love, goodness, compassion, or mercy) is the fourth sĕfīrāh — a masculine active power, corresponding to the right arm of 'Ādām Qadmōn, and whose divine name is *'ēl* (the mighty one).

Gĕbūrāh (strength, power, might), the fifth sĕfīrāh, a feminine potency issuing from and complementing Ḥesed, its masculine counterpart, corresponds to the left arm of 'Ādām Qadmōn. Its divine name is *'elōah* (goddess).

Tif'ereth (beauty, magnificence, glory), the sixth sĕfīrāh, is the fruit of Ḥesed and Gĕbūrāh. It represents the heart of 'Ādām Qadmōn, and is said to be the seat of the sun, from which flows into the surrounding and lower sĕfīrōth all goodness and inspiration. This sĕfīrāh is often termed the Small Countenance or Microprosopus in contradistinction to Kether or Macroprosopus. The divine name of Tif'ereth is *'elōhīm* (divine or mighty ones, gods-goddesses).

Tif'ereth is sometimes called the King (*Melekh*) in connection with Malkhūth as Queen, the tenth sĕfīrāh.

From this second triad or face of the sĕfīrōthal tree, a third triad emanates of still greater heaviness of texture, formed of Netsaḥ, Hōd, and Yĕsōd: Triumph or Firmness, Majesty, and Foundation. *Netsaḥ* (glory, splendor, occasionally time), the seventh sĕfīrāh, is variously translated as Triumph, Firmness, or Subtility. It is the masculine potency representing in archetypal man the right thigh and its divine name is *yĕhovāh tsĕbā'ōth* (lord of hosts or armies).

Hōd (splendor, majesty), the eighth sĕfīrāh, is the feminine potency accompanying the masculine power of Netsaḥ. It represents the left thigh of 'Ādām Qadmōn and its divine name is *'elohīm tsĕbā'ōth*. The *Zohar* states (3:296a) that through Netsaḥ and Hōd "we comprehend extension, multiplication, and force."

Yĕsōd (foundation), the ninth sĕfīrāh, is the fruit or son of Netsaḥ and Hōd. It represents the generative or productive power of 'Ādām Qadmōn. Qabbālāh considered that all energy and life from whatever plane found its portal through Yĕsōd into the manifested world: "All marrow, seed and energy are gathered in this place. Hence all the potentialities which exist go out through this" (Myer, p. 271). Its divine name is *'ēl ḥai* (the mighty living being, lord of life). This name is reminiscent of the Sanskrit term prajāpati, "lord of lives," the progenitor of all living beings on earth.

These six sĕfīrōth, from Ḥesed to Yĕsōd, are termed the sĕfīrōth of construction, partaking of the qualities of manifestation in contradistinction to the supernal triad or unmanifest face of Kether, Ḥokhmāh, and Bīnāh.

The final and tenth sĕfīrāh is named *Malkhūth* (kingdom, dominion), carrier or vehicle of all ten sĕfīrōthal powwers. As Kether is said to contain all the sĕfīrōth in seed, so Malkhūth, its nether pole, is said to express by transmission, as the vehicle, all the superior sĕfīrōth. Representing the feet of archetypal man, it is called also the Bride, Inferior Mother, or Queen, whose symbol is the moon or the earth. Malkhūth represents the close of the spiritual "Construction or Building of the Universe," with which the six sĕfīrōth immediately preceding it were concerned. Its divine name is *'adonāi*, literally meaning not "lord," but "my lords."

Thus have the sĕfīrōth unrolled forth from the Boundless through a series of triads, each of which is progressively more material. Myer sums up the Qabbalistic thought:

> The idea of the Sephiroth is like that of a builder who desires to build a great Palace. 1. He grasps in his mind the plan of the whole building. This is Kether, 'Hokhmah, Binah. 2. Then he considers the way according to which the work shall be done, that it shall correspond to the plan. This is 'Hesed, Tiph'e-reth and Ge'boor-ah. 3. He considers the means of carrying it out, this is Ne-tza'h, Ye'sod and Hod. The entire building is the Divine government of the whole world represented by Malkhuth. — *Qabbalah*, p. 380

Each sĕfīrāh or emanation, proceeding from the top or crown, emanates the one from the other: from the highest comes forth the next highest, from those two, the third, until an invisible triad is formed. Finally all seven manifest sĕfīrōth are formed, no one coming to birth except as the fruit and product of all the preceding ones.

As we have seen, each of the ten sĕfīrōth of 'Ādām Qadmōn — the ideal, cosmic, or archetypal man, the synthesis
of the ten emanations — corresponds to a particular part
of the body. This in no wise should be considered as physi-
calizing spiritual power, but rather as affirming mankind's
intimate relation with divine things, and that even the tenth
emanation carries the mark of celestial and moral potency.
While the correlations of the ten sĕfīrōth with the human
body differ slightly among various writers, the principle
remains the same throughout (cf. Ginsburg, p. 93).

The analogy between the sĕfīrōth and the human body
reflects a cardinal doctrine of the Qabbalists: that everything
that exists in the physical world has its higher and supernal
counterpart in the celestial spheres. So convinced were they
that the body contained planetary and celestial imprints
that they taught it was spirit alone which "produces all the
physiognomies known to the sages."* Hence the early Hebrew initiates venerated the physical body not because of
its material quality, but precisely because it represented to
them the tabernacle or receptacle of divine powers. The
Zohar states:

> as we see in the all-covering firmament stars and planets
> which form different figures that contain hidden things and
> profound mysteries, so there are on the skin that covers our
> body certain figures and lines which are the planets and
> stars of our body. All these signs have a hidden meaning
> and attract the attention of the wise who can read the face
> of man.   — 2:76a, Franck, p. 191

Zohar 2:73b, Franck, pp. 181-3.

4

The Ten Sĕfīrōth in Diverse Forms

THE DEVELOPMENT OF THE TEN SĕFĪRŌTH or "splendors" from 'ein sōf was depicted by ancient and medieval Qabbalists in a multitude of ways. Because the whole truth can never be contained in one symbol, nor even in a score of them, it is in the assembly of various aspects of any one teaching that a larger vision may be attained. This diversity of symbol serves on the one hand to widen and universalize one's comprehension, thus reducing dogmatism; and on the other hand acts as a disciplinary aid to memory development.

In a medieval manuscript of the thirteenth century, unpublished except for portions incorporated by Adolf Jellinek in his *Beiträge zur Geschichte der Kabbala* (Contributions to the History of the Kabbala), Rabbi Isaac of Akko of the School of Segovia gives a series of these illustrations, which we quote from Isaac Myer's translation:*

Illustrations delivered orally, served to explain the mystery

Qabbalah, pp. 251-2, from the manuscript of Rabbi Isaac of Akko: "Enlightenment of the Eyes," *Has-Sēfer Mĕ'ērath 'Ēinayīm.*

of the Unity of the Ten Sephiroth in themselves, which is always concentrated in Ain Soph, from Ain Soph to the Ain Soph. . . . Remember that some of the Qabbalists compare it (the Unity) to a chain forming an uninterrupted unity by its joined links; . . .

This is a graphic symbol of the inner being of planets and stars, described in theosophy as a planetary and/or solar chain of globes. Each sĕfīrāh or "link" (be it globe, planet, or sun) is within its own realm an independent, self-contained entity, composed of its own substance and manifesting its unique character; nonetheless each sĕfīrāh is bound with the whole and with the other sĕfīrōth or "links" in unbreakable unity. In *The Secret Doctrine* (2:23) HPB writes: "In the ancient Cosmogonies, the visible and the invisible worlds are the double links of one and the same chain," i.e., the upper sĕfīrōth and the lower, the "invisible" and the "visible," are all, individually and collectively, links of the one chain.

The second illustration likens the sĕfīrōth "to *various waters issuing from one source*, and separating into many rivers, which become (again) united in the ocean; from whence they return again, from beneath the earth, to their former divisions; and so on in an uninterrupted unity; . . ." (Myer). On this point the *Zohar* says:

The form in which he is generally depicted is to be compared to a very expansive sea; for the waters of the sea are in themselves without a limit or form, and it is only when they spread themselves upon the earth that they assume a form (דמיון [dimyōn]). We can now make the following calculation: the *source* of the sea's water and *the water stream* proceeding therefrom to spread itself *are two*. A great reservoir is then formed, just as if a huge hollow had been dug; this reservoir is called sea, and is *the third*. The unfathomable deep divides itself into *seven streams*, resembling seven long vessels. The source, the water stream, the sea and the seven streams make together *ten*. And when the master breaks the vessels which he has made, the waters return to the source, and then only remain the pieces of these vessels, dried up and without any water. It is in this way that the Cause of Causes gave rise to the *ten Sephiroth*.

— 1:42b, 43a, Ginsburg, p. 95

In this extract we have a profound symbolism: the Waters of Space ('ēin sōf), without form or shape, as soon as the "last vibration of the seventh eternity thrills through infinitude" (*SD* 1:28) spread and take form (*dimyōn*). The source of the Waters, the current or stream of water that flows from it, and the reservoir into which the stream empties, are the three unmanifest sĕfīrōth — Kether, Ḥokhmāh, and Bīnāh — from which issue the seven *kēlīm* (vessels), the seven manifest sĕfīrōth.

Comparing the Qabbalistic statement that "the master breaks the vessels," with a stanza from *The Secret Doctrine*, "Then the sons dissociate and scatter . . ." (1:30), we see two ways of describing the withdrawal of the life-hosts from the world or chain of worlds for the period of dissolution which follows each period of activity or manifestation. "The waters return to their source," but not the vessels, the vehicles which the life-waves use, are cast off and broken into pieces, yet the essences endure and "return to their source" as the *Zohar* says; or as the Stanzas of Dzyan have it, they "return into their mother's bosom at the end of the great day, and re-become one with her."

In the third illustration,

> others compare the matter of the union of Mercy and Se-verity [the two opposing Pillars of sĕfīrōthal power] to a *precious stone* which unites in itself, the various peculiarities of other precious stones of different qualities (colours?) and still remains a perfect unity; ... — Myer, pp. 251-2*

The myriad facets of the one precious stone remind one of a title of the Buddha — "diamond heart" — which signifies that the Buddha or "awakened one" had so polished and perfected the seven (ten or twelve) facets of his constitution that his whole nature is crystal-clear. The power of this symbol is not so much in the perfection of one or more facet(s), but in the symmetry of the whole, in the interplay of each to each, of each to the whole: each part subordinate to the whole, and yet each part essential to the integrity of the whole.

Fourthly, "others, take as an illustration, the unity of the different colors in *the flame proceeding from a burning coal*, in which, both flame and coal, constitute a unity; ..." (Myer). This symbol is frequently used in the *Zohar*, as well as in the *Sēfer Yĕtsīrāh*. The *Zohar* further states:

> In order to acquire the knowledge of a holy unity, we must examine the flame which rises from a fire-place or from a lighted lamp; we see then, at first, two kinds of light, a glis-tening white one and a black or blue one; the white light is above and rises in a straight line, the black or blue light is beneath, and appears to be the seat of the first; yet the two

lights are so closely united that they form one single flame only. But the seat formed by the blue or black light is, in its turn, attached to the wick which is still under it. The white light never changes, it always remains white; but several shades are distinguished in the lower light. The lower light takes, moreover, two opposite directions; above it is attached to the white light, and below it is attached to the burning matter, but this matter continually consumes itself, and constantly rises towards the upper light. It is thus that all that is joins again to the one unity.

— 1:51a, Franck, pp. 166-7

Note the sentence that contains the essence of Zoharic thought: "The white light never changes, it always remains white; but several shades are distinguished in the lower light" — i.e., Kether, the first emanation or first Logos, does not change while the lower sĕfirōth are distinguished by the variety in quality of their individual lights.

For the fifth illustration, Isaac of Akko chose "the simile of *a bunch of grapes*, in which both bunch and grapes are one" (Myer). The symbolism is universal: that of the wine of the spirit inherent in every aspect of nature. While each grape is a discrete entity, by itself it constitutes nothing permanent; when combined, the bunch then suggests a complete sĕfirōthal tree, the unity of diverse elements.

In the sixth illustration, Isaac of Akko states:

I have furthermore heard from the mouth of the most prominent of our learned men, the metaphor of *the tree with its roots* (the Ten Sephiroth) in the earth and its numerous branches, twigs, leaves, veins, fruits, and their rinds and kernels, which all are derived from each other, and yet all draw from the marrow of the tree, and thus all collectively form a complete and unbroken unity, from the roots to the very top of the tree, because they all are of, and point to, one and the same essential source.   — Myer, p. 252

As we have seen, the tree of life or lives, *'ēts ḥayyīm*, is described variously in the *Zohar*: at one time with its roots in the earth and its branches ascending spiritwards, as recorded by Isaac of Akko; at other times "as a tree having its roots in heaven, the trunk and branches being the several Sephiroth" (Myer, p. 253); and still again as a "Tree of Life Below" which reflects a "Tree of Life Above," as in the following:

> But while it is permitted to reveal, now is the time to reveal it, that all the *Neshamoth* [plural of Nĕshāmāh] souls, go out from that great Tree and from that mighty River which flows out from Eden, and all the *Ru'hin* [plural of rūaḥ] spirits come out from that other small tree. The *Neshamah* soul, comes from Above, the *Rua'h* spirit, from Below, and unite in one . . . and nothing is ever lost. — 2:99b, Myer, p. 413

> Above in the Tree of Life exist no strange *Q'lippoths* [shells] for it is said: "With Thee dwelleth no Evil" (Ps. v, 5) but in the Tree, Below, exist the strange *Q'lippoths*.
> — 1:27a, Myer, p. 436

Another variant of the great tree is seen in the following extract from the *Zohar*:

> This Tree goes up to the heavenly clouds and it is hidden between three mountains. From under the three mountains, the Tree goes out and ascends to the Above and comes down to the Below. This House is supplied by it with drink, and there is hidden in it (that House) many hidden things

Above, which are not known. This Tree is revealed in the daytime and covered (hidden) in the night.

— 1:172a, Myer, p. 385

The symbol of the tree of life or lives under whatever form is one of the most ancient. It plays an important part in the great world religions, especially when represented as a tree with its roots placed in the spiritual worlds, its branches descending into matter. The following quotations from *The Secret Doctrine* illuminate this Zoharic concept:

The Norse Ask, the Hesiodic Ash-tree, whence issued the men of the generation of bronze, the Third Root-Race, and the *Tzite* tree of the *Popol-Vuh*, out of which the Mexican *third* race of men was created, are all one. This may be plainly seen by any reader. But the Occult reason why the Norse Yggdrasil, the Hindu Aswatha, the Gogard, the Hellenic tree of life, and the Tibetan Zampun, are one with the Kabalistic Sephirothal Tree, and even with the Holy Tree made by Ahura Mazda, and the Tree of Eden — who among the western scholars can tell? Nevertheless, the fruits of all those "Trees," whether Pippala or Haoma or yet the more prosaic apple, are the "plants of life," in fact and verity. The prototypes of our races were all enclosed in the microcosmic tree, which grew and developed *within and under* the great mundane macrocosmic tree, . . .   — 2:97

The tree *was reversed*, and its roots were generated in Heaven and grew out of the Rootless Root of all-being. Its trunk grew and developed, crossing the planes of Pleroma, it shot out crossways its luxuriant branches, first on the plane of hardly differentiated matter, and then downward till they touched the terrestrial plane. Thus, the Asvattha, tree of Life and Being, whose destruction alone leads to immortality, is said in the Bhagavatgita to grow with its roots above and its branches below (ch. xv). The roots represent the Supreme Being, or First Cause, the LOGOS; but one has to go beyond those roots to *unite oneself with Krishna*, who, says Arjuna (xi.), is "greater than Brahman, and First Cause . . . the indestructible, that which is, that which is not, and what is beyond them.". . . He only who goes *beyond* the roots shall never return, *i.e.*, shall reincarnate no more during this "age" of Brahmā.

It is only when its pure boughs had touched the terrestrial mud of the garden of Eden, of our Adamic race, that this Tree got soiled by the contact and lost its pristine purity; . . . — 1:406

Still other analogies for the ten sĕfīrōth are found in the various books of the *Zohar*. A seventh illustration compares them to sparks produced from the anvil or "by steel from the flint, which are always hidden in the latter as a potency and unity, and brought into visibility only by friction" (Myer, p. 252). This has reference in a broad sense to the emanation of "lives," whether of humans or worlds, from ʼēin sōf; and specifically to the "sparks" which were "old worlds which were destroyed." The sparks or scintillae are the myriads of imbodying lives which flash forth from ʼēin sōf. Compare this with the Stanzas of Dzyan:

From the effulgency of light — the ray of the ever-darkness — sprung in space the re-awakened energies; . . . And these are the essences, the flames, the elements, the builders, the numbers [i.e., the sĕfīrōth], the arupa, the rupa, and the force of Divine Man [ʼĀdām Qadmōn] — the sum total. And from the Divine Man emanated the forms, the sparks, . . . — *SD* 1:30

As regards the particular sense in which the *Zohar* refers to the "sparks" being "ancient worlds which were destroyed," the *Hā-'Idrā' Zūṭā' Qaddīshā'* (The Small Holy Assembly) states:

421. And therefore were the Prior Worlds destroyed, for the Prior Worlds were formed without (*equilibrated*) conformation.

422. But these which existed not in conformation are called vibrating flames and sparks [*zīqīn nītsōtsīn*], like as when the worker in stone striketh sparks from the flint with his hammer, or as when the smith smiteth the iron and dasheth forth sparks on every side.

423. And these sparks which fly forth flame and scintillate, but shortly they are extinguished. And these are called the Prior Worlds.

424. And therefore have they been destroyed, and persist not, until the Most Holy Ancient One can be conformed, and the workman can proceed unto His work.

— Mathers, p. 301

Many were the attempts to build the worlds, but each was unsuccessful until the Holy Ancient One had assumed control, by producing a "balance" (*mathqĕlā'*) between the spiritual and material, for only then could the sĕfīrōthal tree of lives endure. As the sixth Stanza of Dzyan says:

The older wheels rotated downward and upward. . . . The Mother's spawn filled the whole (*Kosmos*). There were battles fought between the Creators and the Destroyers, and battles fought for Space; the seed appearing and reappearing continuously. — *SD* 1:199

HPB comments:

The phrase "Older wheels" refers to the worlds or Globes of our chain as they were during the "previous Rounds." The present Stanza, when explained esoterically, is found embodied entirely in the Kabalistic works. Therein will be found the very history of the evolution of those countless Globes which evolve after a periodical Pralaya, rebuilt from old material into new forms. The previous Globes disintegrate and reappear transformed and perfected for a new phase of life. In the Kabala, worlds are compared to sparks which fly from under the hammer of the great Architect — LAW, the law which rules all the smaller Creators. — Ibid.

Another illustration presents the sĕfīrōth as a series of concentric circles or spheres, with Kether at the outermost and Malkhūth at the center. The accompanying diagram (between pp. 54-5) of the ten sĕfīrōth arranged as a series of concentric circles or spheres is both ancient and profound, for the circle (or egg or sphere) has from immemorial antiquity been revered as a symbol of continuous and ever-becoming life. HPB writes:

The Spirit of Life and Immortality was everywhere symbolized by a circle: . . . The incorporeal intelligences (the Planetary Spirits, or Creative Powers) were always represented under the form of circles. In the primitive philosophy of the Hierophants these *invisible* circles were the prototypic causes and builders of all the heavenly orbs, which were their *visible* bodies or coverings, and of which they were the souls. It was certainly a universal teaching in antiquity. (See *Ezekiel*, ch. 1.)

"Before the mathematical numbers," says Proclus (*in Quinto Libro* EUCLID), "there are the *Self-moving* numbers; before the figures apparent — the vital figures, and before producing the material worlds *which move in a Circle*, the Creative Power produced the *invisible* Circles."

— *SD* 2:552

Substituting the term sĕfīrōth for planetary spirits or creative powers in HPB's reference, or again in Proclus' for the words "numbers" and "figures," gives an accurate picture of the Qabbalistic approach — which is not strange at all because, if sprung from the same source, each of the world systems of thought ought to prove identic in essentials.

The correlation imbodied in the diagram of the planetary and cosmic influences with the ten sĕfīrōth is patterned after the generally accepted listing given by most Qabbalistic writers, though slight differences in order are observable among them. In considering the correlation of the seven sacred planets (*shib'āh kōkhābīm*) with the sĕfīrōth, the significant point is not the actual order but the continual interaction of spiritual, intellectual, psychical, and physical energies among the zodiac, sun, and planets with our earth, or among the globes of a planetary chain.

The symbol of concentric spheres is not peculiar to Zoharic thought: it is found in many cultures. For example, in the Sumerian and Babylonian cosmogonies, it survives in the ziggurats or stepped pyramids where each story represents a different planet. It is found in Greek thought under various forms, notably in the teaching of the "crystalline spheres" enunciated by Eudoxus of the fourth century BCE, where the planets were described as

hollow, transparent globes enclosed one within the other and surrounding the quiescent body of the earth; first,

the "primum mobile," which carried around all the inner spheres and communicated to them a universal motion, next a sphere for all the stars, then one for the sun, one for the moon, and one for each of the five planets then known.
— *The Romance of Astronomy: The Music of the Spheres*
by Florence Armstrong Grondal, p. 199

A ninth illustration of the sĕfīrōth is archetypal man within an ovoid sphere, where the various members of the human body are depicted as corporeal representatives of the ten cosmic sĕfīrōth. While this is a graphic symbol, it tends to anthropomorphize the original cosmic conception of the celestial and planetary oneness with man as a living flame, as a compound of spiritual, intellectual, and vital fires. When these elements are included in the diagram of the concentric circles, their universal aspect is apparent: the ten lights or splendors are viewed at one and the same time as the cosmic, solar, and planetary spheres; the seven or ten globes of a planetary chain; the ten numbers issuing from no-number,* as well as the ten elements of the body.

A tenth illustration depicts the sĕfīrōth as a nut, the kernel of which is the "light," sheathed in a series of shells or rinds, which are the "envelopes" or "palaces" surrounding that light. After comparing the world to a nut whose kernel is enwrapped in a series of shells, the *Zohar* says:

> It is even thus with the entire universe, superior and inferior; from the mysterious superior point, as far as the extremity of all the Degrees (Sephiroth), all form one whole; of which the parts are formed, one in the other, insomuch that they

---

*Cf. Stanza 4, *SD* 1:30-1.

serve as shells, the one to the other. The first point (the Sephirah Kether, the Ego or Will) was an interior and incommensurable Light, so that we are not able to know its splendour, subtility and purity, until (we reach) that which has developed itself by expansion. That expansion of the point, becomes a temple or palace, enveloping this same point, that is, the Light which we cannot know because of its great splendour. But that palace (Sephirah) which serves as the envelope of that occult point, is itself an incommensurable Light, without containing equally the same subtility and splendour, as the first concealed and occult point. That sphere is again extended through a new expansion (forming) a first Light, an expansion which serves as an envelope of that subtile sphere (which is) clear and altogether interior. The portions of existence continued thus to develope, the one from the other, and to envelope themselves the one in the other. So that they each and in totality, served as mutual envelopes, and that they (relatively the one to each and to all the others), are as the kernel and the shell, but yet all are one in totality, because that which is one envelope, is at the same time, a kernel for another degree. All absolutely occurs the same in these inferior regions; and man in this world is made after that resemblance, being (composed) of a kernel and a shell, which are the spirit and the body. Such is in general the order of the universe. — 1:19b-20a, Myer, pp. 190-1

In an eleventh illustration, the sĕfīrōth are pictured as a lightning flash, in its turn shooting forth flames; or again as a series of "immeasurable lights" or "splendors." The *Sēfer Yĕtsīrāh* says: "Ten are the sephiroth out of the Void whose appearance is like a flash of lightning" (1:5). In the portion of the *Zohar* entitled *Hā-'Idrā' Zūṭā' Qaddīshā'* (The Small

Holy Assembly) occur several passages where the sĕfīrōth are compared to a series of lights, flames, or splendors:

74. He the Eternal Ancient of the Ancient Ones is the highest Crown among the Supernals, wherewith all Diadems and Crowns are crowned.

75. And from Him are all the Lights [sĕfīrōth] illuminated, and they flash forth flames, and shine.

76. But He verily is the Supreme Light, which is hidden, which is not known.

77. And all the other Lights are kindled by Him, and derive (their) splendour (from him). . . .

85. Furthermore, the Most Holy Ancient One is symbolized and concealed under the conception of the Unity, for He himself is One, and all things are One.

86. And thus all the other Lights are sanctified, are restricted, and are bound together in the Unity or Monad, and are One; . . .   — Mathers, pp. 267-8

The above illustrations by no means exhaust the fund of Qabbalistic imagery. So fertile was their inventive power, and so profoundly imbued were they with this conception of the sĕfīrōthal energies pouring forth from the Boundless — 'ēin sōf — the Qabbalists read into even the most ordinary human affairs the symbol of the tree of life. They even compared the unrolling of the sĕfīrōth to peeling the skins of an onion, the layers of the skin, etc.

The predominant thought throughout symbol, diagram, and metaphor was, as HPB expressed it, that "All these personified Powers are not evolutions from one another, but so many aspects of the one and sole manifestation of the

ABSOLUTE all" (*SD* 1:350). Or again, as Krishna explained
to Arjuna:

> Although (I am) unborn, of imperishable selfhood, al-
> though (I am) lord of all beings, yet while abiding in my
> own natural state, I take birth through the illusion of self
> (i.e., I take birth by my own power — *ātmamāyayā*).
>
> — *Bhagavad-Gītā*, ch. 4, śl. 6

5

The Triadic Nature of the Sĕfīrōth

THE TEN SĔFĪRŌTH ARE DIVIDED into triads of various types, or into two Faces, the Great Face (Macroprosopus) and the Little Face (Microprosopus). The triadic nature of the sĕfīrōth manifests as three heads and three divisions of archetypal man, as well as three worlds (*'ōlāmīm*) or faces (*'anpīn*).

The first of the three heads is itself triadic, composed of Kether, Ḥokhmāh, and Bīnāh: Kether in this context being the crown of the head; Ḥokhmāh the wisdom of the brain; and Bīnāh the understanding that comes from the heart. The main consideration in the mind of the Qabbalist was that the three highest sĕfīrōth should stand for the highest qualities in 'Ādām Qadmōn, hence for the head and heart combined in wisdom, which three-in-one forms the head of 'Ādām Qadmōn. *Hā-'Idrā' Zūṭā' Qaddīshā'* states:

> 78. He the Most Holy Ancient One ['attīqā' qaddīshā']
> is found to have three heads, which are contained in the one
> Head.
> 79. And He Himself is that only highest supreme Head.
> — Mathers, p. 267

The succeeding sĕfīrōth likewise form into triads, patterning themselves after the supernal triad. *Hā-'Idrā' Zūṭā' Qaddīshā'* continues:

> 80. And since He the Most Holy Ancient One is thus symbolized in the Triad, hence all the other Lights which shine are included in Triads. — Ibid.

Thus another triad issues from the upper one, composed of Ḥesed (or Gĕdūlāh) and Gĕbūrāh (or Dīn or Paḥad),* the two arms, and Tif'ereth, the heart, which together form the chest of 'Ādām Qadmōn. From this middle triad, a third and lowest triad is produced, composed of Netsaḥ and Hōd, the two limbs, with Yĕsōd the generative power, together forming the Foundation of 'Ādām Qadmōn.

These three triads — the Head, the Chest, and the Foundation — pour their energies into and hence manifest through the lowest or tenth sĕfīrāh, Malkhūth, the Kingdom, known as the Feet or Stability of 'Ādām Qadmōn.

These heads or divisions have, each one, its presiding ruler: the first head or triad is governed by Kether; the second by Tif'ereth; and the third by Yĕsōd (or Malkhūth). Connecting these three with the diagram of the concentric spheres correlating the sĕfīrōth with the planetary and cosmic influences, we see that Kether, ruler of the supernal triad, represents Primum Mobile, the primordial motion, the divine breath, the first quiver of manifestation; that Tif'ereth, the ruler of the second triad, stands for the sun, giver of spiritual, intellectual, and vital life; that Yĕsōd, ruler

---

*Gĕdūlāh is an alternate name for Ḥesed, and means greatness, might, power; Dīn and Paḥad are alternate terms for Gĕbūrāh and signify judgment, and fear, awe, or justice.

of the lowest triad, represents the moon, giver of psychical and physical life; while Malkhūth, the Kingdom in which the three rulers govern, represents the foundation or elements, our earth, the vehicle and carrier of the divine, solar, and lunar forces.

These three triads parallel the three *upādhis* or bases which form the human constitution. In *Fundamentals*, Purucker writes:

> Man can be considered as a being composed of three essential bases; the Sanskrit term is *upādhi*. The meaning of the word is that which "stands forth" following a model or pattern, as a canvas, so to say, upon which the light from a projecting lantern plays. It is a play of shadow and form, compared with the ultimate reality. These three bases or upādhis are, first, the monadic or spiritual; second, that which is supplied by the lords of light, the so-called mānasa-dhyānis, meaning the intellectual and intuitive side of man, the element-principle that makes man man; and the third basis or upādhi we can call the vital-astral-physical, if you please.
>
> These three bases spring from three different lines of evolution, from three different and separate hierarchies of being. . . .
>
> . . . The lowest comes from the earth, ultimately from the moon, our cosmogonic mother; the middle, the mānasic or intellectual-intuitional, from the sun; the monadic from the Monad of monads, the supreme flower, or acme, or rather the supreme seed of the universal hierarchy which forms our cosmical universe or universal cosmos. — p. 152

We thus see right down the sĕfīrōthal tree of lives a center pillar of divine, solar, lunar, and terrestrial power pouring through Kether, Tif 'ereth, Yĕsōd, and Malkhūth, and correspondingly energizing in the human constitution nĕshāmāh, rūaḥ, nefesh, and gūf.

When these three worlds are viewed as faces (*'anpīn* or *partsūfīn*), then Kether is called the Supernal Face; Tif 'ereth is called the King (*Melekh*, Aramaic *Malkā'*) or the "Sacred King" (*Malkā' Qaddīshā'*); Malkhūth (or Yĕsōd) is the Queen, the Bride of Melekh, and is called Malkhĕthā', Maṭrōnā', or Maṭrōnīthā', the "Matron" or "Mother." This last correspondence is significant. We have mentioned that there were "prior worlds," "ancient worlds," which could not subsist because the Sacred Ancient had not "assumed its form," in other words because the King and Queen, Tif 'ereth and Yĕsōd-Malkhūth, had not united to produce the "balance" (*mathqĕlā'*) essential for the sĕfīrōthal tree to live. In still other words, the sun and moon had not yet united their energies to produce the earth with its hosts of living beings — a statement applicable to the genesis of worlds, the birth of humankind, and the awakening of the human soul to its spiritual possibilities.

Malkhūth in very truth is the Kingdom: the receiver and carrier of every one of the nine superior sĕfīrōthal powers, each of the three sĕfīrōth of the right and left pillars respectively contributing its individual power through the presiding ruler of the three triads or faces, so that the central pillar, formed of the rulers (Kether, the King, and Queen), focalizes the planetary influences through the three upādhis or bases — the monadic or Kether, the solar or Tif 'ereth, the lunar or Yĕsōd — all finding manifestation in the terrestrial or Malkhūth.

We can also consider the sĕfīrōth as active and passive streams of vitality divided vertically into three currents of energy: the right or masculine Pillar of Ḥesed (compassion or mercy), composed of the three sĕfīrōth on the right: Ḥokhmāh, Ḥesed (or Gĕdūlāh), and Netsaḥ, in which the masculine, transmitting, and centrifugal energies predominate. The left or feminine stream of vitality, which complements the masculine stream, is called the Pillar of Dīn (judgment), composed of the three sĕfīrōth on the left: Bīnāh, Gĕbūrāh or Dīn, and Hōd, in which the feminine, receiving, and centripetal energies predominate.

The third or central current of vitality, the stream of spiritual stability, is called the Center Pillar of Raḥamīm (sympathy or harmony). Composed of the four sĕfīrōth running from Kether vertically through Tif'ereth and Yĕsōd, down to and including Malkhūth, it represents the harmonious interplay between the right and left pillars. It is the stabilizing pillar between the two opposing forces; the right and left, the transmitting and receiving, the centrifugal and centripetal pillars. In other words, in the Center Pillar the planetary energies focused in the right and left pillars of *'ēts ḥayyīm* (tree of lives) are received and stabilized in order to flow down successfully into Malkhūth for manifestation on earth. Along this central stream flow currents in unceasing rhythm from Kether the Crown through the intermediate sĕfīrōth down to the lowest, Malkhūth, and one's consciousness may ascend or descend along this invisible pathway. Because the sĕfīrōthal tree applies not only to the cosmos as a whole, but to every living being as well, this pathway is also within each one of us.

6

The Four Worlds

Far from teaching the existence of one Adam as sole progenitor of humanity, Qabbālāh distinguishes four Adams or humanities, existent on and appropriate to four *'ōlāmīm* (worlds or planes). These Adams range in quality of character from the spiritual or first Adam, the 'Ādām Qadmōn of the *Zohar*, to the lowest or most material, the terrestrial Adam of *Genesis*. Four worlds or planes gradually decreasing in spirituality are described as four extensions or manifestations of the primeval Heavenly Adam.

'Ōlām (singular of *'ōlāmīm*) is from a Hebrew verb signifying originally "to conceal, to hide," with a philosophical extension of meaning of "hidden time," or an age whose birth and death are "concealed" from profane knowledge, but during whose existence spiritual beings "live and move and have their being." In brief, *'ōlām* is a world or condition of being in which entities, human or other, pass a certain portion of time, and thus undergo in space a number of experiences. It is similar in conception to the Sanskrit *loka*, and identic with the Gnostic *aion*.

'Ōlām is the old word for "eternity," often misunderstood to mean forever and ever without end. Originally

it did not connote endless duration; on the contrary, the *Zohar* regards it as a defined period of time during which entities manifest in one or another condition of being — hence a world or sphere.

The four Adams are conceived of not as distinct from the ʿōlāmīm, but rather as their consciousness side. So intimately related are they to one another that the ʿōlāmīm are often termed the Adams, while the four Adams are just as frequently called the four ʿōlāmīm. When viewed from the standpoint of the *entities* who inhabit and inform these worlds or planes, they are called the Adams; when considered as the *worlds* on and in which entities evolve, they are called the ʿōlāmīm. Further, each of the Adams has its own sĕfīrōthal tree of life in and through which it experiences the tenfold qualities of consciousness.

Thus three streams of emanational energy issue forth from the Boundless, ʾēin sōf: (a) the tenfold sĕfīrōthal tree of lives, (b) the four ʿōlāmīm, and (c) the four Adams. Correlating these with the theosophical philosophy, and taking as an instance the manifestation of a planetary chain: (a) the sĕfīrōth would correspond to the varying states of consciousness of the seven (or ten or twelve) globes of such a chain; (b) the ʿōlāmīm to the lokas and talas or the four cosmic planes or worlds on and in which the globes or sĕfīrōth function; and (c) in the human context, the four Adams correspond to the four root-races or humanities of our present planetary life cycle or round of existence. Such correspondences are not hard and fast. Generally speaking, the three Zoharic emanations appear to be the Qabbalistic way of describing what theosophists understand by globes,

THEOSOPHICAL UNIVERSITY PRESS

P O BOX C

PASADENA CA 91109–7107 USA

Our Complete Catalog

may be obtained by filling out this card and returning it to us.

PLEASE PRINT

Mr/Mrs/Ms _____

Address _____

City, State, & Post Code _____

Country _____

Please include information about:

❑ The Theosophical Society   ❑ Correspondence Courses

Visit us online at www.theosociety.org

planes of being, and root-races, each of them distinct, yet intimately related and mutually interdependent like the sides of a triangle.

The four worlds or ʿōlāmīm are considered as four emanations or productions of ʾēin sōf, the Boundless which, "as *it* could not be made manifest, was conceived to emanate manifesting Powers. It is then with its *emanations alone that human intellect has to, and can deal*" (*SD* 2:41). The Qabbalistic names for these four emanations are:

(1) *ʿōlām hā-ʾatstsīlōth*, "world of junction or condensation," sometimes called *ʿōlām has-sĕfīrōth*, "world of emanations or numbers." It is the highest of the four worlds, the junction point between realms of utter spirit above and the increasingly material ʿōlāmīm below. As the prototype or spiritual pattern of the lower worlds, it is the emanator of the other ʿōlāmīm.

(2) *ʿōlām hab-bĕrīʾāh*, "world of production or creation," the vehicle or shell of ʿōlām hā-ʾatstsīlōth, receiving the spiritual energies from above and manifesting them in less fullness than its prototype. This world of production or creation in turn becomes the prototype of the next world in succession.

(3) *ʿōlām hay-yĕtsīrāh*, "world of formation," acts as a vehicle for the creative forces of the second ʿōlām, manifesting them in still decreasing plenitude of spirituality. Nevertheless, this third world acts as prototype to our earth, the lowest of the four ʿōlāmīm.

(4) *ʿōlām hā-ʿaśiyyāh*, "world of action and labor," the field of earthly existence, is the fourth world. It is the vehicle of the third sphere, and hence manifests in still less

fullness the splendor of spirituality. This world has also been called *ʿōlām haq-qĕlīppōth,* "world of shells or rinds," indicating that on our earth only the rinds or shells of reality manifest, while the qualities of the human spirit find themselves in varying degree at home in the upper ʿōlāmīm.

It is interesting that the three lower ʿōlāmīm are called by names whose roots all mean "to form," yet each word imbodies shades of meaning sufficiently different to indicate that form on the plane of bĕrī'āh would be of an intellectual or ideative character, while form on the plane of yĕtsīrāh would be more material, though not as material as that of the lowest world of ʿaśiyyāh. The roots also imply that form on the plane of yĕtsīrāh acts more on the astral world, while that of ʿaśiyyāh has more to do with the condensation of physical matter.

Ginsburg, in his *Kabbalah,* writes about the four ʿōlāmīm:

> The different worlds which successively emanated from the *En Soph* and from each other, and which sustain the relationship to the Deity of first, second, third, and fourth generations, are, with the exception of the first (*i.e.,* the World of Emanations), inhabited by spiritual beings of various grades. . . . the first world, or the Archetypal Man, in whose image everything is formed, is occupied by no one else. The angel METATRON, (מטטרון) [Mĕṭaṭrōn], occupies the second or *the Briatic World* (עולם בריאה) [ʿōlām bĕrī'āh], which is the first habitable world; he alone constitutes the world of pure spirits. He is the garment of שדי [Shaddai], i.e., the visible manifestation of the Deity; his name is numerically equivalent to that of the Lord. (*Sohar,* iii, 231 *a.*)

He governs the visible world, preserves the unity, harmony, and the revolutions of all the spheres, planets and heavenly bodies, and is the Captain of the myriads of the angelic hosts who people the second habitable or *the Jetziratic World* (עולם יצירה) ['ōlām yĕtsīrāh], and who are divided into ten ranks, answering to the *ten Sephiroth*. Each of these angels is set over a different part of the universe. One has the control of one sphere, another of another heavenly body; one angel has charge of the sun, another of the moon, another of the earth, another of the sea, another of the fire, another of the wind, another of the light, another of the seasons, &c. &c.; and these angels derive their names from the heavenly bodies they respectively guard.   — pp. 108-10

Each of the four 'ōlāmīm is held by the *Zohar* to have its locus in the individual human being, each corresponding with one of the four basic principles of the human constitution. Hence nĕshāmāh, spirit, is believed to manifest without hindrance in 'ōlām hā-'atstsīlōth; rūaḥ, spiritual intelligence, finds similar freedom in 'ōlām hab-bĕrī'āh; nefesh in 'ōlām hay-yĕtsīrāh; and gūf, the shell or container of the preceding spiritual, intellectual, and psychic breaths, is in 'ōlām haq-qĕlīppōth.

These 'ōlāmīm do not manifest as descending layers from 'ēin sōf, or like the steps of a ladder, one below the other, but surround one another, as the sheaths of the human constitution may be said to envelop the pearl of nĕshāmāh:

> As in the human organism, the Neshamah the thinking mind, which has its seat in the brain; is surrounded by the Rua'h, a spirit which dwells in the heart; and this by

the Nephesh, the life spirit permeating the entire body; and finally all of these are covered with flesh, skin, bones, and then clothing, so in the construction of the universe, the Makrokosmos, in the highest Sephirothic world, the A'tzeel-oothic, is surrounded by the B'ree-atic world, that of Creation or Emanation, the Soul and expressed Will of the Deity; this by that of Ye'tzeer-ah or world of Formation, *i.e.*, the Life Force, and this finally by the world of Action, A'seey-ah, the world of Corporiety, which is the shell or cover. — *Zohar* 1:20a, Myer, p. 292n

Speaking of the heavens or other earths, the process of emanation is described as follows:

And all the heavens are one above the other, like the layers of an onion, and some Below and some Above, . . . And the Lower earths where do they come from? They are from the chain of the earth and from the Heaven Above.
— *Zohar* 3:9b, 10a, Myer, pp. 415-16

On each of these worlds a complete tenfold tree of life is emanated. While each sĕfīrōthal tree is patterned after the universal plan, nevertheless it manifests its own characteristic energy appropriate to the ʿōlām on which it unfolds. This is alluded to in allegorical fashion:

And there come out from it [any particular world or ʿōlām] different creatures differing one from the other. Some of them in garments (skins), some of them in shells (*Q'lippoth*) like the worms which are found in the earth, some of them in red shells, some in black, some in white, and some from all the colors. — *Zohar* 3:10a, Myer, pp. 416-17

The different colors are reminiscent of the Stanzas of Dzyan

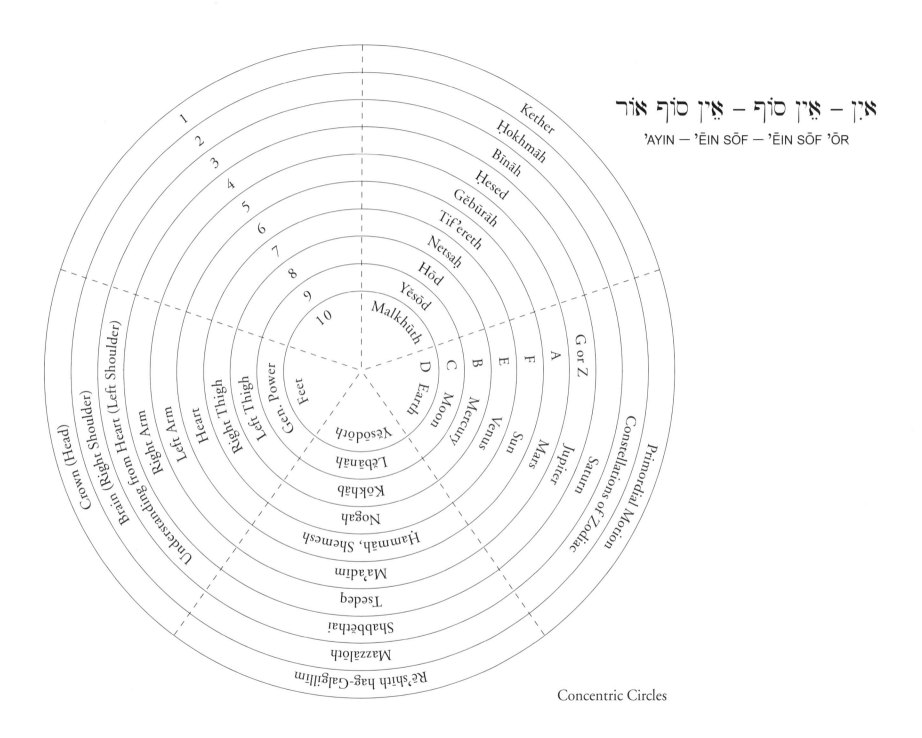

אַיִן – אֵין סוֹף – אֵין סוֹף אוֹר

'AYIN — 'ĒIN SŌF — 'ĒIN SŌF 'ŌR

Concentric Circles

(*SD* 2:20), in which the various human races are termed moon-white, yellow, red, and black — not that the beings manifest on any 'ōlām are *physically* red or white, or any other color, but that such colors suggest varying qualities of development.

Thus (a) each of the four worlds emanates or manifests a sĕfīrōthal tree *in harmony* with the specific quality of the 'ōlām; or (b) viewing the matter from the consciousness side, each of the sĕfīrōthal manifestations conditions the quality of a particular 'ōlām. It is the old problem of deciding whether, in theosophical terminology, the worlds or globes condition the quality of their kingdoms of evolving beings, or whether the lives themselves determine — because emanating the worlds from themselves — the quality and character of such worlds. The latter view is perhaps closer to the esoteric conception, hence we may just as accurately say that each of the four sĕfīrōthal trees in the last analysis emanates or develops its corresponding 'ōlām as its field of action during manifestation.

The following diagram reproduced from *The Secret Doctrine* shows HPB's comparison of the Eastern Gupta-Vidyā (secret wisdom) with the Chaldean Qabbālāh. We have here seven cosmic planes, three of which remain unnamed and undefined because they are of so spiritual and ethereal a quality as to be incomprehensible to our terrestrial intellect. In modern theosophical literature these three higher planes are called *arūpa,* "formless" (a Sanskrit word meaning without a body or form *as we understand it*). But they are just as real and vital in the consciousness of those supernal beings who inhabit and vivify those spheres as our earth is

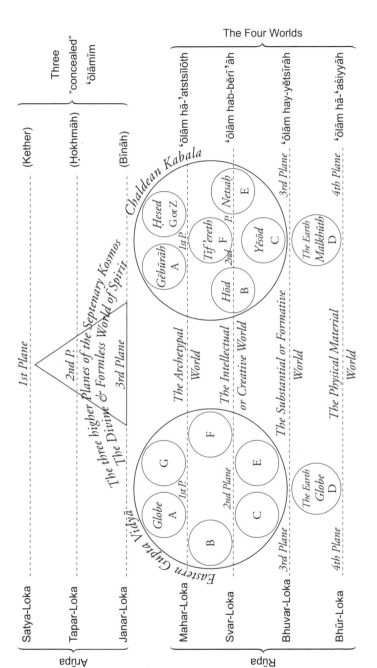

The Four Worlds

Three "concealed" ʿōlāmīm

(Kether) — Satya-Loka

(Ḥokhmāh) — Tapar-Loka

(Bīnāh) — Janar-Loka

ʿōlām hā-ʾatstsīlōth

ʿōlām hab-bĕrīʾāh

ʿōlām hay-yĕtsīrāh

ʿōlām hā-ʿasiyyāh

Chaldean Kabala

Ḥesed G or Z

Gĕbūrāh A

1st P.

Tifʾereth F

Netsaḥ E

Hōd B

2nd P.

Yĕsōd C

The Earth Malkhūth D

The three higher Planes of the Septenary Kosmos
The Divine & Formless World of Spirit

1st Plane

2nd P.

3rd Plane

The Archetypal World

The Intellectual or Creative World

The Substantial or Formative World

The Physical Material World

Eastern Gupta Vidyā

Globe A

G

1st P.

F

B

2nd Plane

C

E

The Earth Globe D

3rd Plane

4th Plane

Mahar-Loka

Svar-Loka

Bhuvar-Loka — 3rd Plane

Bhūr-Loka — 4th Plane

Arūpa

Rūpa

Adapted from *The Secret Doctrine* 1:200

to us. Regarding these invisible spheres, HPB writes: "The three upper are the three higher planes of consciousness, revealed and explained in both schools only to the Initiates, the lower ones represent the four lower planes — the lowest being our plane, or the visible Universe" (*SD* 1:199). These three upper planes, in which the supernal triad of Kether, Ḥokhmāh, and Bīnāh are dominant, cannot be reached by the ordinary consciousness, as the individual "must awaken the three 'seats' to life and activity. And how many are capable of bringing themselves to even a superficial comprehension of *Atma-Vidya* (Spirit-Knowledge), . . ." (ibid.).

For convenience, on the right side of HPB's diagram we have added the Qabbalistic terms for the 'ōlāmīm — the four 'ōlāmīm corresponding with the four manifested planes; and on the left we have placed the lokas in one manner of describing them. Note that the names of the three higher unmanifest lokas are given in Sanskrit literature, and that we do not have the names of the three higher "concealed" 'ōlāmīm. But we do have the names of the three higher sĕfīrōth — Kether, Ḥokhmāh, and Bīnāh — and we may presume that these upper "concealed" 'ōlāmīm were originally known to the initiates who transmitted the ancient Qabbālāh from which its modern child, the Hebrew Qabbālāh, is derived. *The Secret Doctrine* gives a hint of this: "First comes En-Soph, the 'Concealed of the Concealed,' then the *Point*, Sephira and the later Sephiroth; then the *Atzilatic* World, a *World of Emanations* that gives birth to three other worlds . . ." (2:111). We are dealing here with the four lower or manifest planes, the field of the four 'ōlāmīm.

Studying HPB's diagram further, we note the distribution of the seven manifest globes of a planetary chain (as an instance in point of the seven manifest qualities of any being, whether a sun, planet, man, or atom) on the four manifest ʿōlāmīm, two by two on the three higher manifest ʿōlāmīm, and one — the lowest, our earth — on the fourth and most material of the planes.

Further, the globes as thus distributed on the ʿōlāmīm are correlated each to a particular sĕfīrāh: the seven lower or manifest sĕfīrōth corresponding to the seven globes on and in the four cosmic planes. At the same time, on each of the ʿōlāmīm a tenfold sĕfīrōthal tree of life is manifested, which illustrates another facet of this multifaceted conception. What HPB is suggesting in this diagram is that on any specific plane or ʿōlām, *one aspect of consciousness only is dominant at any one time*, all other aspects of the sĕfīrōthal tree being present in potential, but manifesting in *minor* degree.

An old work by the seventeenth-century Jesuit Athanasius Kircher contains an interesting diagram of the sĕfīrōthal tree which indicates that within each sĕfīrāh there are ten sub-sĕfīrōthal powers.* The more modern Qabbalists, however, seem to ignore this point.

If for every sĕfīrāh of the manifested ʿōlāmīm we find a corresponding ʿōlāmic power, we may conclude that for every *sub*-sĕfīrāh there must be a *sub*-ʿōlām. Further, each ʿōlām must then contain *in potentia* the other sub-ʿōlāmic qualities. The following from an article based on Knorr

---

*Cf. *Oedipi Aegyptiacus*, 1652.

von Rosenroth's *Kabbala Denudata* (*Kabbalah Unveiled*) confirms this thought:

> Each of these four worlds is sub-divided into four, and then we read of the Aziluth ['Atstsīlōth] (or Abia) of Aziluth, the Briah [Běrī'āh] of Aziluth, the Jezirah [Yĕtsīrāh] of Aziluth and the Asiah ['Aśiyyāh] of Aziluth; and similarly in the case of the other three.
>
> — "The Kabbala and the Microcosm – I," by Montague R. Lazarus, *The Theosophist*, Sept. 1887, p. 769

Hence, 'ōlām hā-'atstsīlōth is called such not because this 'ōlām alone is present, but because of the four 'ōlāmic qualities existent there, the 'atstsīlōthic power is dominant. Precisely the same with the other 'ōlāmīm: each quality is dominant in its own sphere, while the other three sub-'ōlāmīm are more or less recessive.

The following diagram may help clarify these nuances of Qabbalistic thought. We note the four 'ōlāmīm or planes of consciousness descending in serial order from the spiritual, through the second and third, until the world of physical matter, our earth, is reached.

The second 'ōlām we will now examine in detail. Here we have 'ōlām hab-běrī'āh expanded into four *sub*-'ōlāmīm, correlated to the *sub*-sěfīrōth of the sěfīrāh native to this 'ōlām (Tif'ereth), as well as the corresponding *sub*-global aspects of globe F of the earth-chain, coeval with Tif'ereth. From this threefold correlation, some interesting points develop:

(a) The three highest sěfīrōth — above the seven manifested sěfīrōth on the four manifested planes — imply three

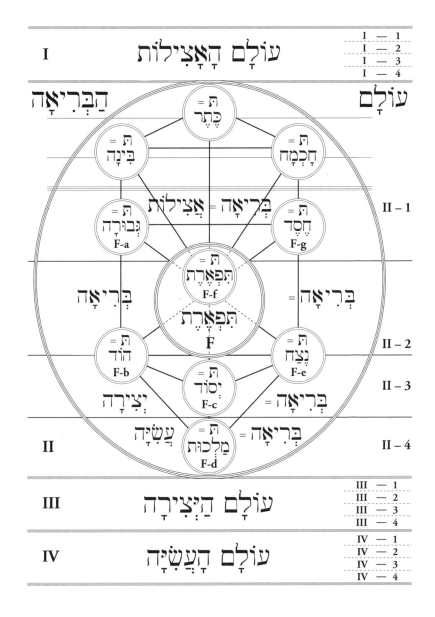

עוֹלָם

הַבְּרִיאָה

כֶּתֶר = תּ

בִּינָה = תּ   חָכְמָה = תּ

בְּרִיאָה = אֲצִילוּת

גְּבוּרָה = תּ
F-a

חֶסֶד = תּ
F-g

II – 1

תִּפְאֶרֶת = תּ
F-f

בְּרִיאָה   תִּפְאֶרֶת   בְּרִיאָה =

F

הוֹד = תּ
F-b

נֶצַח = תּ
F-e

II – 2

יְסוֹד = תּ
F-c

בְּרִיאָה =

II – 3

יְצִירָה

עֲשִׂיָּה = תּ   בְּרִיאָה =

מַלְכוּת = תּ
F-d

II

II – 4

Sub-ʿŌlāmīm

higher planes on which to function, i.e., three higher "concealed" ʿōlāmīm on and in which the three highest of the sĕfīrōth function;

(b) the three highest sĕfīrōth similarly suggest three higher globes of a planetary chain. From this we may conclude that ʿōlām hab-bĕrīʾāh expands to contain: (1) three concealed or superspiritual ʿōlāmīm; (2) three concealed or superspiritual global qualities; and (3) three concealed or superspiritual sĕfīrōth.

The existence of these three subfactors within this second manifested cosmic plane points out that *within every* ʿōlām there must likewise exist the same series of concealed or superspiritual sub-ʿōlāmīm, sub-sĕfīrōth, and sub-global characteristics — a veritable hierarchy of "concealed" divinely spiritual powers, the inner unrevealed source of the manifested ʿōlāmīm.

The sub-ʿōlāmīm of the world of Bĕrīʾāh have already been described; the sub-sĕfīrōth and sub-globes correlated to them are:

Sub-ʿōlāmīm	Sub-sĕfīrōth	Sub-globes
Bĕrīʾāh-ʾAtstsīlōth	Tifʾereth-Ḥesed	F-g
"	-Gĕbūrāh	F-a
Bĕrīʾāh-Bĕrīʾāh	" -Tifʾereth	F-f
"	-Hōd	F-b
Bĕrīʾāh-Yĕtsīrāh	" -Netsaḥ	F-e
"	-Yĕsōd	F-c
Bĕrīʾāh-ʿAśiyyāh	" -Malkhūth	F-d

In this regard, we quote a few lines from a medieval manuscript of Ḥayyīm Vital, the most beloved and important disciple of Isaac Luria, which presents the procession of the ʿōlāmīm and sĕfīrōth as sparks of scintillating light coming forth from ʾēin sōf:

The Ten Sephiroth of A'tzeel-ooth [ʾAtstsīlōth] have scintillated and brought forth the Ten Sephiroth of B'ree-ah [Bĕrī'āh], and from the energy of these Ten of B'ree-ah, sparkled forth the scintillations of the World Ye'tzeer-ah [Yĕtsīrāh], and through these, the Ten Sephiroth of the World A'seey-ah [ʿAśiyyāh] were sealed . . .

— ʿĒts Ha-Ḥayyīm, "Tree of Life," fol. 253, col. 2, Myer, p. 331

The Four Adams

THE FOUR ADAMS FOLLOW THE same plan of development as the four ʻōlāmīm: each becomes both prototype or pattern for the succeeding Adam, and reflection or image of the preceding Adam; the highest being prototype alone, while the lowest serves solely as reflection or image of the higher Adams.

> The lower world is made after the pattern of the upper world; every thing which exists in the upper world is to be found as it were in a copy upon earth; still the whole is one.
> — *Zohar* 2:20a, Ginsburg, p. 104

This statement coincides with the axiom given in the Smaragdine Tablet of Hermes Trismegistus: "That which is below is like that which is above, and that which is above is like that which is below, for the performance of the miracles of the one substance" (Mathers, p. 155n).

While it is true that the highest Adam acts as the divine-spiritual prototype for the subsequent Adams of the lower ʻōlāmīm, this first Adam (ʼĀdām Qadmōn) is the image or reflection (*tselem*) of "previous worlds" or humanities which had been conceived and destroyed until the world or Adam of Balance (*mathqĕlāʼ*) was formed. Similarly, the lowest or fourth Adam is not solely the reflection of the preceding Adams, but itself acts as prototype for worlds or humanities below it in the realms of *Shě'ōl*, the Underworld.

The first Adam, called *'Ādām Qadmōn* (Eastern or Ancient Adam) or *'Ādām 'Illā'āh* (Highest or Supreme Adam), is likewise termed the 'Atstsīlōthic 'Ādām as it corresponds to and informs the highest world, 'ōlām hā-'atstsīlōth. It is the prototype (*tsūrāh*) of the second and succeeding Adams, the model on which the three lower Adams are built. It corresponds to něshāmāh in the human being.

The second Adam, called the protoplastic androgyne,* is termed the Běrī'atic 'Ādām as it corresponds to and informs 'ōlām hab-běrī'āh. The reflection of the tsūrāh of 'Ādām Qadmōn, it becomes in turn the prototype of inferior degree to the succeeding Adam. It corresponds to rūaḥ in the human constitution.

The third Adam, called the pre-terrestrial or "innocent" Adam, is referred to as the Yětsīrātic 'Ādām, as it corresponds to and informs 'ōlām hay-yětsīrāh. It is the reflection of the tsūrāh of the Běrī'atic 'Ādām, and in turn becomes the prototype of the fourth or lowest Adam of our earth, ordinary humanity. It corresponds to nefesh in the human constitution.

The fourth Adam, the terrestrial Adam of *Genesis*, corresponds to and informs our earth, the lowest of the 'ōlāmīm. This Adam is the reflection of the third Adam, and hence is the feeble reflection, three times removed, of the divine-spiritual tsūrah of the primeval Adam resident on 'ōlām

---

*See Myer, 418-19.

hā-ʾatstsīlōth. In other words, the luminosity of ʾĀdām Qadmōn is progressively dulled one-quarter as its reflection passes through each succeeding Adam, until our fourth humanity perceives but one quarter of truth and in its folly believes it sees reality in full. As far as the earth chain is concerned, these four Adams correspond to globes A, B, C, and D.

Note the identity of conception between the Qabbalistic four Adams and four ʿōlāmīm with the four yugas or "ages." According to the latter, the spirit of truth and light as it manifests in time and space is likened to a bull. In the highest or satya-yuga (truth age), which corresponds to ʿōlām hā-ʾatstsīlōth and ʾĀdām Qadmōn, the bull of dharma stands firm on four legs. In the second or tretā-yuga (threefold age), corresponding to ʿōlām hab-bĕrīʾāh and the Bĕrīʾātic ʾĀdām, truth loses one-fourth of its brilliance, so the bull stands on only three legs. In the third or dvāpara-yuga (twofold age), corresponding to ʿōlām hay-yĕtsīrāh and the third Adam, two parts of truth retire, leaving the bull of truth with but two legs. In the fourth or kali-yuga, corresponding to ʿōlām hā-ʿaśiyyāh and the terrestrial Adam, three quarters of truth have departed, leaving the bull with but a single leg to stand on: one quarter of wisdom, one quarter of light.

Obviously the bull of dharma does not lose its legs one by one, nor does truth depart in the ratio of 4, 3, 2, 1; rather, human perception of primeval truth becomes veiled in proportion as we descend through the spheres and clothe ourselves with the "coat of blindness" of each succeeding ʿōlām. Truth is one and the same throughout time: crystal-clear and whole to the Adam of the highest ʿōlām; proportionally indistinct and fractional to each Adam on its descent to the lowest ʿōlām.

This concept is also reminiscent of the series of ages taught by the Greeks, Hesiod in his *Theogony* among them, as descending in spiritual brilliance from the highest or Golden Age, through the second, Silver Age, the third, Bronze Age, until the lowest or fourth age is reached, called the Iron Age, for so blinded and heavy has the humanity of this last age become.

In discussing the ʿōlāmīm, we reckoned that the original Qabbālāh envisioned the existence of three higher "concealed" ʿōlāmīm corresponding to the highest three sĕfīrōth. It follows that, if for each of the four manifest ʿōlāmīm there is a corresponding Adam, there must be concealed or higher Adams corresponding to the higher and concealed ʿōlāmīm. Consider again our diagram of the sub-ʿōlāmīm on page 60, where we expanded one ʿōlām to contain a complete sĕfīrōthal tree unfurled on the three unmanifest or concealed ʿōlāmīm and the four manifest or lower ʿōlāmīm. Substituting the Adams for the ʿōlāmīm in this diagram, illustrates the above.*

Further, if what applies to the ʿōlāmīm likewise pertains to the several Adams, then just as each ʿōlām has its sub-ʿōlāmic powers, so each of the Adams itself contains in degree the potencies of the other three Adams. For example, in the highest Adam, ʾĀdām Qadmōn is the dominant energy, with the other three sub-Adamic powers recessive and but

---

*See *SD* 2:46 reference to "seven primordial Adams."

partially expressed. In the second Adam, 'Ādām Qadmōn remains in fullness, but emanates the second or Bĕrī'ātic 'Ādām, which then becomes dominant — like Krishna, who "establishes this universe with a portion [of himself], and yet remains separate." Similarly with the third and fourth Adams.

In correlating the four Adams with the four root-races as outlined in theosophical writings, we must not consider only the physical standpoint. In fact, the major significance lies in the *spiritual* transformation from 'Ādām Qadmōn, through the descending spheres, to the Adam and Eve of present humanity. The *physiological* conversion from the homogeneous Adam of the first 'ōlām, through the proto-plastic androgynous state of the second Adam, to the sexed humanity of today is of secondary importance, being not the cause but a by-product of fundamental evolutionary courses. According to HPB:

> The original Kabala was entirely metaphysical, and had no concern with animal, or terrestrial sexes; the later Kabala has suffocated the divine ideal under the heavy phallic element. — *SD* 2:457

She reminds us further that

> Esotericism ignores both sexes. Its highest Deity is sexless as it is formless, neither Father nor Mother; and its first manifested beings, celestial and terrestrial alike, become only gradually androgynous and finally separate into distinct sexes. — *SD* 1:136n

'Ādām Qadmōn, therefore, as the chief or hierarch of the first manifested beings, celestial and terrestrial alike, is not just the first Adam of the first world, but imbodies within its cycle all that goes with the beginning of a new appearance or manifestation of worlds and humanities out of the ages-long past. Thus, 'Ādām Qadmōn is the archetype of succeeding forms. The "World of Perfect Ideas," as Qabbālāh phrases it, is equivalent to the third or manifested Logos in theosophy through which, as a focus or laya-center,* flow all the seeds of the lives to come. These seeds of future worlds and humanities are contained within 'Ādām Qadmōn not as *physical* elements, but as spiritual energies "in their true form," the *diyyūqnā'* or "spiritual counterpart." As the *Zohar* has it:

> when this last work was nigh completion, all the things of this world, all the creatures of the universe, in whatever age they were to exist, before ever they entered into this world, were present before God in their true form.

> — 3:61b, Ginsburg, p. 104; cf. also Myer, p. 388

In short, the archetypal form was impressed on the plastic substance of the divine seeds, which later expressed themselves in manifestation on earth.

In the process of emanation from the Boundless, the *Zohar* refers to several unsuccessful attempts to form a universe. Before the ten sĕfīrōth were emanated in their present form, several elementary worlds suffered birth and death, until at length the sĕfīrōth of perfect balance came forth successfully from the womb of space and time:

> There were old worlds which perished as soon as they came

---

*Dissolution point between two planes of consciousness or matter.

into existence: were formless, and they were called sparks.
... These sparks are the primordial worlds, which could not
continue, because the Sacred Aged had not as yet assumed
his form (of opposite sexes — the King and Queen), and the
master was not yet at his work.

— *'Idrā' Zuṭā'*, *Zohar* 3:292b, Ginsburg, p. 103

Finally the "Aged of the Aged" assumed a form in which
it could manifest its full capacities and powers. The four
Adams and four ʿōlāmīm, therefore, were not the first
worlds to take shape, but the offspring or fruit of a series of
evolutionary efforts:

Before the Aged of the Aged, the Concealed of the
Concealed, expanded into the form of King, the Crown of
Crowns (*i.e.* the first *Sephira*), there was neither beginning
nor end. He hewed and incised forms and figures into it
in the following manner: — He spread before him a cover,
and carved therein kings (*i.e.*, worlds), and marked out their
limits and forms, but they could not preserve themselves.
... All these were imperfect: he therefore removed them
and let them vanish, till he finally descended himself to this
cover and assumed a form.

— *'Idrā Rabbā'*, *Zohar* 3:148a, Ginsburg, p. 103

The *Zohar* frequently refers to these "previous worlds"
as the Kings of Edom who "reigned before the monarchs"
and who were then destroyed "since they had not as yet the
perfect form of which they were capable" (3:135b, Ginsburg,
pp. 102, 104). It may be significant that the word Edom
(*'edom*) has the same consonants in Hebrew as the word
Adam (*'Ādām*): 'Ālef, א, dāleth, ד, and final mēim, ם. These
worlds or kings may also refer to periodical obscurations, as

well as to "the several continents which have disappeared, as also their decline and geographical change of place" (*SD* 2:705), likewise to the destruction of early races, until fit vehicles were produced to retain the sacred form, the kingly or mānasaputric energy from the sun.

In answer to the question: "Why were these primordial worlds destroyed?" the *Zohar* states:

> Because the Man, represented by the ten *Sephiroth*, was not as yet. The human form contains every thing, and as it did not as yet exist, the worlds were destroyed. . . . Still when it is said that they perished, it is only meant thereby that they lacked the true form, till the human form came into being, in which all things are comprised, and which also contains all those forms. — 3:135b, Ginsburg, p. 104

HPB comments:

> Worlds and men were in turn formed and destroyed, *under the law of evolution* and *from pre-existing material*, until both the planets and their men, in our case our Earth and its animal and human races, became what they are now in the present cycle: opposite polar forces, an equilibrized compound of Spirit and Matter, of the positive and the negative, of the male and the female. Before man could become male and female *physically*, his prototype, the creating Elohim, had to arrange his Form on this sexual plane *astrally*. That is to say, the atoms and the organic forces, descending into the plane of the given differentiation, had to be marshalled in the order intended by Nature, so as to be ever carrying out, in an immaculate way, that law which the Kabala calls the *Balance*, through which everything that exists does so as male and female in its final perfection, in this present stage

of materiality. . . . Therefore the First Root-race of men, sexless and mindless, had to be overthrown and "hidden until after a time"; *i.e.*, the first race, instead of dying, disappeared *in the second race*, as certain lower lives and plants do in their progeny. It was a wholesale transformation. The First became the Second Root-race, without either begetting it, procreating it, or dying. "*They passed by* together," as it is written: "And he died and another reigned in his stead." (*Genesis* xxvi, 31 *et seq. Zohar* iii., 292 *a*) Why? Because "the *Holy City* had not been prepared." — *SD* 2:84

Hence 'Ādām Qadmōn, as the receptacle of the seeds of future lives, is not only the prototype (*tsūrāh*) of the lower manifestations, but de facto the radiant "image" (*tselem*), the consummation, of "previous worlds." Here the tselem corresponds to the Sanskrit word *chāyā* as used by HPB in *The Secret Doctrine*: in the tselem of the 'elohīm was 'Ādām made (*Zohar* 3:76, Cremona ed.), in the image of the ancestors or pitris mankind was fashioned (cf. *Genesis* 1:27). Not only "in the image," however, but also of the substance of this tselem was humanity formed; in other words, the human ancestors projected their astral forms which became the lower principles of the individual members of the human race.

Further, 'Ādām Qadmōn could in no sense be "the creative origin of all things, which is composed of the Host of Cosmic Powers — the Creative Dhyan-Chohans" (*SD* 1:443), unless previous karmic ties enabled it to gather from the spaces of 'ēin sōf those "seeds of beings" which belong to it by right of attraction, impelled thence by links of spiritual, intellectual, psychomagnetic, and physical destiny.

'Ādām Qadmōn is therefore the tsūrāh of the lower worlds, not as their *originator* but as *transmitter* of ancient yet ever evolving powers-to-be. HPB describes this specific function of 'Ādām Qadmōn:

> the celestial Logos, the "Heavenly Man" ['Ādām Qadmōn or 'Ādām 'Illā'āh], which evolves as a Compound Unit of Logoi, out of whom after their pralayic sleep — a sleep that gathers the ciphers scattered on the Mayavic plane into One, as the separate globules of quicksilver on a plate blend into one mass — the Logoi appear in their totality as the first "male and female" or Adam Kadmon [in his manifest aspect], the "Fiat Lux" of the Bible, . . . But this transformation did not take place on our Earth, nor on any material plane, but in the Spacial Depths of the first differentiation of the eternal Root-matter.　　— *SD* 1:246

'Ādām Qadmōn is often called simply by the name of its genius or rector, the presiding influence of that world, termed *diyyūqnā'*, "spiritual form or counterpart": the world of "perfect form or will" (Myer, p. 332).

The second Adam, which corresponds to the second root-race, is called the protoplastic androgyne because the spiritual and material poles of evolution (i.e., the *noumena* of masculine and feminine potencies, not their *physical* manifestations) have begun to individualize while still remaining unified in one field of activity. This Běrī'ātic 'Ādām is likewise referred to by its "presiding influence" or rector, called *kūrsěyā'*, the "throne" occupied by Měṭaṭrōn, the "great teacher" or angel of this second world, the "abode of pure spirits."

Metatron governs the visible world, preserves the unity, harmony and revolutions of the spheres, planets and all the heavenly bodies; and is the Commander, under the Will of the Deity, of all the myriads of the angelic hosts, of the next or Ye'tzeer-atic World.   — Myer, p. 328

In the *Zohar* the "presiding influence" or genius of the third Adam is called *mal'ākhayyā',* the "angels" or "messengers," called the "abode of the Angels, the Intelligences of the Celestial planets and stars" (ibid.). The same world is sometimes termed the "Living Ones" (*Ḥayyōth*). The preterrestrial or "innocent" Adam corresponds to that period of our racial history where spirit and matter, masculine and feminine, active and passive, become distinctly specialized, but where egoic self-consciousness of the opposing energies is still unawakened. When the children of this third Adam "eat of the fruit of the Tree of Knowledge of Good and Evil," the work of the 'elohīm or mānasaputras, the sons of intelligence, is accomplished, and the third Adam or third humanity envelops the "cloak of the higher light" (*'ōr*) of previous Adams with the "coat of skin" (*'ōr*), the coat of flesh and blindness.*

As the *Zohar* says:

> He gave supernal wisdom to Adam, but Adam utilised the wisdom disclosed to him to familiarise himself with the lower grades also, until in the end he attached himself to the *yetzer-hara* (evil tempter), and the fountains of wisdom were

---

*Note the difference in 'ōr, אוֹר, meaning light and 'ōr, עוֹר, meaning skin, also by extension, blindness, matter. The numerical value of א ('ālef) is One, of ע ('ayin) is seventy.

closed to him. After he repented before his Master, parts of that wisdom were again revealed to him, in that same book, but through that same knowledge people came later on to provoke God. — *Zohar* 1:75b, 76a, Sperling 1:257

The feminine potency having now become too strong to be contained within the sphere of the masculine, in other words the differentiation or specialization of the two poles having matured, Eve is drawn out of the side or rib (*tsēlā'*) of Adam, and the third Adam, now become Adam and Eve, step(s) out of the Garden of Eden (*Gan-'Ēden*) into the valleys of matter, the home of the fourth or terrestrial Adam of *Genesis*. One could, of course, just as well say that man was separated from woman, or made from a rib or side of woman, since Adam signifies not one individual male person, but the whole of androgynous humanity.

This last Adam corresponds to the fourth or most material root-race, and is clothed not only with a "coat of skin" or blindness, but hides within, deep enough to be hid from human knowledge, the "cloaks of the higher light" of the upper ethereal Adams:

God clothed Adam and Eve in garments soothing to the skin, as it is written, He made them coats of skin (*'or*). At first they had had coats of light (*'or*), which procured them the service of the highest of the high, for the celestial angels used to come to enjoy that light; so it is written, "For thou hast made him but little lower than the angels, and crownest him with glory and honour" (Ps. viii, 6). Now after their sins they had only coats of skin (*'or*), good for the body but not for the soul. — *Zohar* 1:36b, Sperling 1:136

The "presiding influence" of this fourth Adam is *Sammā'ēl*, who rules over the *'ōfannīm* (the "wheels" of birth and death) and the *galgillīm* or *gilgūlīm* (the "revolutions" of the planetary spheres). Called the Angel of Death and Prince of Darkness or of Poison, Sammā'ēl rules the seven habitations called *shĕba' hēikhālōth*, which are the seven infernal or material zones of our globe, the lower seven of the ten degrees which make the dwelling places of beings inhabiting the lowest 'ōlām. This fourth world is divided into ten degrees, as reflections of the sĕfīrōthal tree, and these are divided into three higher or relatively immaterial spheres and seven material or infernal regions. HPB correlated Sammā'ēl with desire, kāma, emphasizing his duality as both the evil knowledge of the Tree of the Knowledge of Good and Evil and pure spirit divorced from form. The Talmud states that "the evil Spirit, Satan, and Sammā'ēl the Angel of Death, are the same"; and Sammā'ēl's role is made equivalent to that of the serpent in the *Genesis* account of Eve tasting of the fruit of the Tree of Knowledge of Good and Evil. He is also termed the chief of the Dragons of Evil, and in conjunction with Lilith is represented as the Evil Beast (*ḥiwyāi' bīshā'*).

'Ādām Qadmōn, then, as the "chariot" (*merkābāh*) or carrier of all the seeds of previous worlds gathered from 'ēin sōf, manifests as four individualized entities, each entity or root-race finding appropriate expression in the sĕfīrōthal tree on its respective 'ōlām. Two lines of evolution thus proceed simultaneously: (a) the retirement of spiritual capacity, the "cloaks of the higher light," in the intensification of material pursuit of the descending Adams; and (b) the expan-

sion or evolution of a physical vehicle or "coat of skin" for
the spiritual powers to manifest through. From the union
of these two, energized by the sons of intelligence or 'elohīm, self-conscious thinking humanity is born. As HPB
describes it:

> The Occult Doctrine teaches that while the monad is cy-
> cling on downward into matter, these very Elohim — or
> Pitris, the lower Dhyan-Chohans — are evolving *pari passu*
> with it on a higher and more spiritual plane, descending also
> relatively into matter on their own plane of consciousness,
> when, after having reached a certain point, they will meet
> the incarnating senseless monad, encased in the lowest mat-
> ter, and blending the two potencies, Spirit and Matter, the
> union will produce that terrestrial symbol of the "Heavenly
> Man" in space — PERFECT MAN.   — *SD* 1:247

The sons of the fourth Adam, ourselves, must *self*-con-
sciously become that "Heavenly Man." We must choose
between the "cloaks of the higher light" which call us upwards, and the "coats of blindness" which drag us continuously down to material things. The former influences us for
good, the latter for evil. This interplay of forces affects the
destiny of every one of us, as individual and racial units, and
on this theme the *Zohar* has much to say:

> When our forefather Adam inhabited the Garden of Eden,
> he was clothed, as all are in heaven, with a cloak of the
> higher light. When he was driven from the Garden of Eden
> and was compelled to submit to the needs of this world,
> what happened then? God, the Scriptures tell us, made for
> Adam and his wife coats of skin and clothed them; for before
> this they had coats of light, of that higher light used in Eden.

. . . The good actions accomplished by man on earth draw upon him a part of that higher light which shines in heaven. It is this light which serves him as garment when he is to enter into another world and appear before the Holy One, Whose name be praised. Thanks to this garment he is able to taste the bliss of the elect, and to look into the luminous mirror. That it may be perfect in all respects, the soul has a different garment for each of the two worlds it is to inhabit, one for the earthly world, and one for the higher world.

— 2:229b, Franck, p. 208

8

Symbolism of 'Arīkh 'Anpīn and Zĕʿēir 'Anpīn

Kᴇᴛʜᴇʀ, ᴛʜᴇ ꜰɪʀsᴛ sᴇ̆ꜰꜰ̄ʀᴀ̄ʜ, called the open eye in contrast to 'ēin sōf, the closed eye, is the Ancient of Days ('attīq yōmīn), the Old Man of the Zohar who produces from the cranium of his White Head the three sĕfīrōthal triads which manifest through Malkhūth, the tenth sĕfīrāh. In three books of the Zohar — Sifrā' di-Tsĕnī'ūthā' (Book of Concealment), Hā-'Idrā' Rabbā' Qaddīshā' (The Great Holy Assembly), and Hā-'Idrā' Zūṭā' Qaddīshā' (The Small Holy Assembly) — an intricate mystical symbolism is worked out whereby the cranium, hair, eyes, ears, nostrils, mouth, and beard, as well as the other components of the Ancient of Days, are used to illustrate the coming forth into manifestation of the tenfold powers of a sĕfīrōthal tree from the infinitude of 'ēin sōf.

One of the fundamental tenets of the archaic wisdom-religion is that the universe is a living sentient being, and that all within the universe is likewise living and evolving. So profoundly were the Qabbalists imbued with this fact of nature, that they portrayed the universe as a Heavenly Man, 'Ādam Qadmōn, whose head reaches to heaven, and whose feet rest upon the earth.

In all the illustrations or symbols of 'Ādam Qadmōn

— synthesis of the tenfold sĕfīrōthal tree — one feature predominates: the gradation of power from the spiritual to the material. This division into upper and lower, superior and inferior, great and small, is depicted in the *Zohar* as two faces: the Great Face (*'Arīkh 'Anpīn*) and the Small Face (*Zĕ'ēir 'Anpīn*), often referred to by their Graeco-Latin equivalents of Macroprosopus and Microprosopus respectively. As *Hā-'Idrā' Rabbā' Qaddīshā'* (*'Idrā' Rabbā'*) puts it:

> And He Himself, the Most Ancient of the Most Ancient Ones, is called ARIK DANPIN [*'Arīkh 'Anpīn*], the Vast Countenance, or Macroprosopus; and He Who is more external is called ZOIR ANPIN [*Zĕ'ēir 'Anpīn*], or Him Who hath the Lesser Countenance (*Microprosopus*), in opposition to the Ancient Eternal Holy One, the Holy of the Holy Ones. — 5:54, Mathers, pp. 117-18

Sometimes 'Arīkh 'Anpīn is described as *Kether 'elyōn*, the "highest crown," from which the remaining nine smaller crowns derive, these nine inferior sĕfīrōth collectively forming Zĕ'ēir 'Anpīn. More generally, however, 'Arīkh 'Anpīn represents the unity of the three highest sĕfīrōth: Kether, the crown of the head; Ḥokhmāh, the wisdom of the concealed brain; and Bīnāh, the understanding that issues from the heart — a three-in-one.

When 'Arīkh 'Anpīn stands for Kether alone, Zĕ'ēir 'Anpīn is considered to comprise the nine lower sĕfīrōth. When 'Arīkh 'Anpīn represents the superior triad as one energy, Zĕ'ēir 'Anpīn embraces the two remaining triads, the six sĕfīrōth presided over by Tif'ereth, the Sacred King, while Malkhūth, the tenth and lowest of the sĕfīrōth, stands as the receiver of all the superior powers, and hence is called the Queen, the Bride of Zĕ'ēir 'Anpīn.

Whether divided as one and nine, or three and six (or seven), the same relationship exists: 'Arīkh 'Anpīn is the prototype, Zĕ'ēir 'Anpīn the reflection; phrased otherwise, 'Arīkh 'Anpīn is the originator and spiritual progenitor of Zĕ'ēir 'Anpīn, which latter could not exist except as the prolongation and expansion in manifestation of its supernal parent. In the words of *'Idrā' Rabbā'*:

> Now take ye your places, and apply the science (*the Qabalah*) to describe how the parts of Microprosopus are conformed, and how He is clothed with His conformations, from the forms of the Ancient of Days ['Arīkh 'Anpīn], the Holy of the Holy Ones, the Withdrawn of the Withdrawn ones, the Concealed one of All (25:508).
>
> But the conformations of Microprosopus are disposed from the forms of Macroprosopus; and His constituent parts are expanded on this side and on that under a human form, so that there may be manifest in Him the Spirit of the Concealed One in every part (25:510).
>
> The ordering of all things is from the Ancient of Days. For before that He was disposed in His conformation, nothing could be ordained, because as yet it was first necessary that Himself should be ordained; and all the worlds were desolate (26:518).　　— Mathers, pp. 173, 175

Note that the terms previously given for Kether are used interchangeably to denote 'Arīkh 'Anpīn; therefore Ancient of Days ('attīq yōmīn) and Holy of the Holy Ones all refer to Macroprosopus. *Hā-'Idrā' Zūṭā' Qaddīshā'* (*'Idrā' Zūṭā'*) echoes the teaching:

He the Eternal Ancient of the Ancient Ones is the highest Crown among the Supernals, wherewith all Diadems and
Crowns are crowned.

And from Him are all the Lights illuminated, and they
flash forth flames, and shine.

But He verily is the Supreme Light, which is hidden,
which is not known.

And all the other Lights are kindled by Him, and derive
(*their*) splendour (*from him*). — 2:74-7, Mathers, p. 267

In *Sifrā' di-Tsĕnī'ūthā'* (Book of Concealment) an intriguing verse occurs: "The Ancient One ['Arīkh 'Anpīn] is
hidden and concealed; the Microprosopus [Zĕ'ēir 'Anpīn] is
manifested, and is not manifested" (4:1, Mathers, p. 91). In
these few words is the symbolism of the doctrine of *arūpa*
and *rūpa** worlds or spheres of consciousness. 'Arīkh 'Anpīn, the synthesis of the three higher planes or sĕfīrōth, is
"without form" when viewed from below, that is, from the
standpoint of the remaining sĕfīrōth; hence it is "hidden
and concealed" to the consciousness of the lower sĕfīrōth.
Zĕ'ēir 'Anpīn, described above as "manifested" and yet "not
manifested," being the totality of the six (or seven) inferior
sĕfīrōth, is "with form" (rūpa), that is manifest and revealed
as compared with 'Arīkh 'Anpīn, the unmanifest or arūpa.
Within its own range of consciousness, however, Zĕ'ēir
'Anpīn partakes of both manifest and unmanifest qualities:
from the viewpoint of Malkhūth, the lowest of the sĕfīrōth,
the two triads immediately preceding and superior to it in
quality are "not manifest" but "hidden," because invisible,

---

*Sanskrit *arūpa*, "without body"; *rūpa*, "with body."

not apparent *to it*; yet considered from the angle of 'Arīkh 'Anpīn, the whole of Zĕ'ēir 'Anpīn is apparent, manifested, and clothed in vehicles of matter of varying gradation.

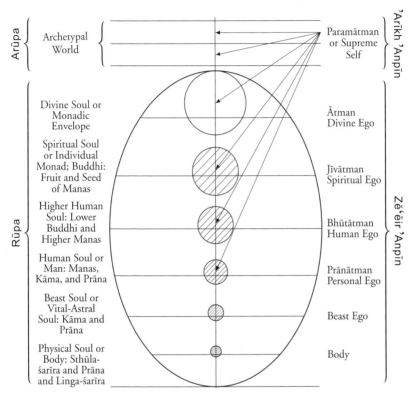

Adapted from *Fundamentals*, p. 240

A diagram in *Fundamentals of the Esoteric Philosophy* illustrates the theme of arūpa and rūpa worlds. As G. de Purucker explains:

> Let the three parallel lines drawn above the egg represent, if you will, the arūpa world, the formless world; and

the seven planes comprised within the egg, the rūpa world, seven being the number of the principles always in manifestation, held in union as an individual by the higher triad, the arūpa triad, its root above.

The three higher of the seven within the egg are also called arūpa, formless, but only relatively so. . . .

. . . through this egg-shaped paradigm falls the ray from the arūpa world, represented by the vertical line signifying the self universally manifesting in every atom it touches in this kosmos — and it permeates them all — as the self individual, the self egoic, the human self, the astral self, etc.

These three highest divisions, the arūpa triad, collectively are likewise called the Paramātman, the supreme self, the summit or flower of the hierarchy, the root-base or source of that self.   — pp. 240-41

In Qabbalistic terms, the three parallel lines stand for the three formless sĕfīrōth (relatively speaking, of course) — Kether, Ḥokhmāh, and Bīnāh — synthesized as 'Arīkh 'Anpīn, the Great Face, the supreme self, equivalent to the Sanskrit paramātman. The six circles within the egg are the six inferior sĕfīrōth of Zĕ'eir 'Anpīn, while the egg itself is the *Shĕkhīnāh*, the "dwelling place" or "vehicle" in and through which all the energies from 'Arīkh 'Anpīn and Zĕ'eir 'Anpīn find expression.

Shĕkhīnāh is an important concept in Jewish mystical thought, being the cloud of glory surrounding a spiritual manifestation. When used in a cosmic sense it is termed the superior Shĕkhīnāh. It then stands for the first divine substance which emanates from 'ēin sōf and envelops it as a veil, from which proceeds the hierarchy of the sĕfīrōth. This corresponds to the Sanskrit parabrahman and mūlaprakṛiti, from which proceed the hierarchies of the manifested universe. In this context the superior Shĕkhīnāh is equivalent to Aditi or Devamātṛi, mother of the gods, and to Vāch, the Voice or Verbum; also to the Pythagorean music of the spheres and the Holy Ghost in the Christian Trinity. The inferior Shĕkhīnāh is associated with the tenth sĕfīrāh — Malkhūth, the material or physical universe. But whatever the stage of manifestation, there is always a radiance enveloping it. We may speak of a Shĕkhīnāh enveloping the human being: our vital aura, the carrier of our higher principles. Qabbālāh regards Shĕkhīnāh as feminine. HPB remarks:

so it is considered in the *exoteric* Purānas, for Shekinah is no more than *Śakti* — the female double or lining of any god, in such case. And so it was with the early Christians whose Holy Spirit was feminine, as Sophia was with the Gnostics. But in the transcendental Chaldean Kabala or "Book of Numbers," "Shekinah" is sexless, and the purest abstraction, a State, like Nirvana, not subject or object or anything except an absolute PRESENCE.

Thus it is only in the anthropomorphised systems (such as the Kabala has now greatly become) that Shekinah-Sakti is feminine. As such she becomes the *Duad* of Pythagoras, the two straight lines of the symbol that can never meet, which therefore form no geometrical figure and are the symbol of matter. Out of this Duad, when united in one basic line of the triangle on the lower plane (the upper Triangle of the Sephirothal Tree), emerge the Elohim, or Deity in *Cosmic* Nature, with the true Kabalists the *lowest* designation, translated in the Bible "God."   — *SD* 1:618-9

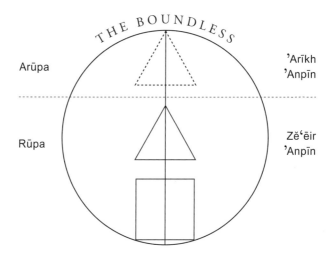

Adapted from *Fundamentals*, p. 125

In a similar diagram from *Fundamentals*, the conception is almost identic, and Purucker's remarks are equally applicable to both diagrams:

> Surrounding this immense spiritual aggregate, we are taught to conceive an aura, as it were, taking the shape of an egg, which we can call, following the example of the Qabbalists, the *Shechīnāh*, a Hebrew word meaning "dwelling" or "vehicle" or what the esoteric philosophy calls the auric egg in the case of man, and representing in this paradigmatic scheme the universe which we see around us in its highest aspects, for this aura is the very outgrowth of Mūlaprakriti [primordial homogeneous substance]; while this mystical line which we draw in the figure as running down through all the various grades of the hierarchy is the stream of the self, the Unconditioned Consciousness, welling up in the inmost of everything. — p. 126

This "stream of the self . . . welling up in the inmost of everything" is 'Arīkh 'Anpīn or Kether, the source of all manifestations. Without the supernal crown, no smaller crowns could derive their splendor, as Qabbālāh phrases it, as all things, whether worlds, humans, or atoms, exist only because they are rays of and from Kether, the divine source, the link with 'ēin sōf. As *'Idrā' Rabbā'* has it: "manifest in Him [is] the Spirit of the Concealed One in every part" (25:510, Mathers, p. 173).

In its manifested aspect, Shĕkhīnāh refers to the tenth sĕfīrāh, Malkhūth, called the Queen or the Mother (Maṭrōnīthā'), the Bride of Zĕ'ēir 'Anpīn, so named because it is

an egg-shaped container or "carrier" or vehicle, an auric egg; and this auric egg, as the tenth, is called Kingdom, or sometimes Dwelling Place, because it is the fruit or result or emanation or field of action of all the others, manifesting through these different planes of being.

— *Fundamentals*, p. 88

To illustrate more graphically the "formless" nature of 'Arīkh 'Anpīn in contrast with the body-character of Zĕ'ēir 'Anpīn, the *Zohar* represents the former as a head alone, while the latter is conceived of as a full-membered being. Hence 'Arīkh 'Anpīn was called White Head (*Rēishā' Ḥiwwārā'*), from whose shining cranium, concealed brain, open eye, nostrils, mouth, and beard, a stream of spiritual force flowed down into Microprosopus, Zĕ'ēir 'Anpīn, who was portrayed as having all the features of 'Arīkh 'Anpīn in inferior proportion, with the remaining members added:

> Of this Most Holy Ancient One, Concealed with all Concealments, there is no mention made, neither is He found.
>
> For since this Head is the supreme of all the supernals, hence He is only symbolized as a head alone without body, for the purpose of establishing all things.
>
> — 'Idrā' Zūṭā' 7:168-9, Mathers, p. 276

The structure and conformations (*tiqqūnīn*) of the Great and Small Faces are fascinatingly described in three books of the *Zohar*. In *Sifrā' di-Tsĕnī'ūthā'* the theme is greatly condensed, making it a more esoteric presentation than that given in *'Idrā' Rabbā'* or *'Idrā' Zūṭā'*, in which Rabbi Shim'ōn, called by his pupils the Lightbearer, illumines the bare outline of the teaching with descriptive illustration. He admonishes his pupils to study well and make true interpretation: "For now wisdom requireth that ye judge a true judgment, becoming and honourable; so that ye may dispose all the conformations as accurately as possible" (*'Idrā' Rabbā'* 25:509, Mathers, p. 173). As in all cases, however, where truth has been submerged in a sea of metaphor, it is not always easy to determine the most exact interpretation, nor is it wise to push analogy beyond truthful limit. No interpretation is put forward here as the only one.

In *'Idrā' Rabbā'* it is written:

> And this is the tradition: The Absolute desired within Himself to create the essence of light, hidden for two thousand years, and produced Her. And She answered thus unto Him: "He who wisheth to dispose and to constitute other things, let Him first be disposed according unto a proper conformation."
>
> — 3:35, Mathers, p. 115

What is the Absolute spoken of above? Is it the Boundless, 'ēin sōf, the limitless fields of space? Or is it the "first and primordial point," Kether, 'Arīkh 'Anpīn — names for the first quiver of manifested life, the first Logos? The latter surely, for the Absolute here is the hierarch or "Sacred Head or Beginning," the *absolutus*, the one "absolved," i.e., freed from the spell of matter and māyā as far as its own hierarchy is concerned. In the words of Purucker:

> The absolute self, our Father in Heaven, is but the Absolute of our hierarchy, its crown, its summit, its glory; or, considering it as the beginning of manifested beings, the root or the seed thereof.   — *Fundamentals*, p. 229

"The Absolute desired" (*sālīq bi-rĕ'ūthā'*) — this is more exactly translated as the "Highest with will (or desire or pleasure)," the Aramaic phrase pointing directly to the age-old teaching expressed by Norsemen, Brāhmans, and Qabbalists alike, that the universe was brought into being through will, through desire, through joy. As the Norse cosmogony expresses it: "Allfather, the Uncreated, the Unseen, dwelt in the depth of the abyss and willed, and what he willed came into being" (*Asgard and the Gods*, p. 22).

The Vedic verse has it : "Desire [kāma, the driving force of love] — first arose in IT." Again, Brahmā — the demiurge, the Evolver — is said to fashion the worlds through the help of *līlā*, "sport" or "play," in other words to have formed all beings and things through the sheer joy infilling his being, which joy overflowed into the forms of manifested lives. Our English word "illusion" bears the same connotation, etymologically as well as philosophically, from *ludo*, "to play," i.e., Deity dreams a dream, in play, and the universe is born.

In the Hebrew Bible Job is challenged as to where he was in the dawn time of the world when "as one the stars of the morning sang, and all the sons of the 'elohīm shouted for joy" (38:7).

Conformations of 'Arīkh 'Anpīn

Before 'Arīkh 'Anpīn ('Ādām Qadmōn, the Qabbalistic Brahmā) could produce the worlds from within himself, the archetypal pattern had to be outlined, so that the inferior might reflect the supernal in proper conformation or arrangement. This "proper conformation" of 'Arīkh 'Anpīn so that he could "constitute other things" is the basis of the conformations, structures, and arrangements which Zĕ'ēir 'Anpīn follows.

In the Mantuan Codex of *Sifrā' di-Tsĕnī'ūthā'* (cf. Mathers, pp. 45-6), the conformations of 'Arīkh 'Anpīn are given as the seven conformations of the skull (*gūlgaltā'*) of the White Head. Other Qabbalistic writers make no such definite allocation, but whatever the numbering or arrangement of these conformations, the general correspondence of Macroprosopus with the arūpa or nonmanifest worlds remains.

Following the system of the Mantuan Codex for purposes of illustration, these seven conformations of gūlgaltā' are: (1) the skull itself, *gūlgaltā'*; (2) the dew, *ṭallā'*; (3) the aetheric membrane or skin, *qĕrūmā' dĕ'awwēirā'*, surrounding the "hidden wisdom" (*ḥokhmĕthā' sĕthīmā'āh*) or supernal brain (*mōḥā' 'illā'āh*); (4) the hair, *nīmā'*; (5) the forehead, *mitshā'*; (6) the open eye, *'einā' pĕqīhā'*; and (7) the nose or nostrils, *hōṭāmā'*. From these seven hangs the beard (*dīqnā'*), itself divided into thirteen conformations, four representing those belonging strictly to 'Arīkh 'Anpīn and nine inferior ones pertaining to Zĕ'eir 'Anpīn (Mathers, pp. 67, 81-2).

The Skull: First Conformation

In *'Idrā' Rabbā'* it is written:

> Into forty thousand superior worlds the brightness of the skull of his Head is extended, and from the light of this brightness the just shall receive four hundred worlds in the world to come (3:41).

> Within His skull exist daily thirteen thousand myriads of worlds, which draw their existence from Him, and by Him are upheld (3:43).

> And from that skull issueth a certain white shining emanation, towards the skull of Microprosopus, for the purpose of fashioning His head; and thence towards the other inferior skulls, which are innumerable.

> And all the skulls reflect this shining whiteness towards the Ancient of Days, . . . (5:56-7).

> The whiteness of this skull shineth in thirteen carved out sides: in four sides from one portion; in four sides from the part of His countenance; and in four sides from another part of the periphery; and in one above the skull, as if this last might be called the supernal side (5:52).

— Mathers pp. 116-18

'Idrā' Zūṭā' describes gūlgaltā' thus:

> The skull of the White Head hath not beginning, but

its end is the convexity of its joining together, which is extended, and shineth.

And from it the just shall inherit four hundred desirable worlds in the world to come.

And from this convexity of the joining together of this White Skull daily distilleth a dew into Microprosopus, into that place which is called Heaven; and in that very place shall the dead be raised to life in the time to come.

— 2:51-3, Mathers, pp. 264-5

Gūlgaltā', the skull of 'Arīkh 'Anpīn, inclusive of the other six conformations contained within it, imbodies the theosophical conception of *Brahmāṇḍa*, a Sanskrit word meaning egg of Brahmā, generally rendered "world egg." In the *Zohar* gūlgaltā' is not only the skull in the sense of the hard shell of the world egg, but comprises the entire contents of the world egg itself as the container of the germs of the "forty thousand superior worlds of brightness" which "wheel" or "revolve" (*gālal*) into manifested existence, i.e., which issue from 'Arīkh 'Anpīn down through Zĕ'ēir 'Anpīn, and from the latter "towards the other inferior skulls which are innumerable," into Malkhūth. These worlds are the archetypes of the future manifested worlds: solar systems, planets, and indeed the innumerable hosts of life-waves or kingdoms of beings which flourish on these worlds from the most spiritual and evolved down to the lowliest and most material in evolution.

"The whiteness of the skull," the "white shining emanation," and also the "worlds of brightness" are equivalent to *hiraṇyagarbha*, a Sanskrit word signifying "golden womb," "egg of light," described in the Stanzas of Dzyan (3:4, *SD*

1:66) as the "luminous egg . . . which in itself is three," i.e., 'Arīkh 'Anpīn, the synthesis of Kether, Ḥokhmāh, and Bīnāh; or again as the "Golden Womb, Hiranyagarbha — which is the Mundane Egg or sphere of our Universe"; and still again compared with Prajāpati (the progenitor of lives) from which emanate the three concealed and the seven manifested spheres.

> The Prajāpati are, like the Sephiroth, only seven, including the synthetic Sephira of the triad from which they spring. Thus from Hiranyagarbha or Prajāpati, the *triune* (primeval Vedic Trimurti, Agni, Vayu, and Surya), emanate the other seven, or again ten, if we separate the first three which exist in one, and one in three, all, moreover, being comprehended within that one "supreme" Parama, called Guhya or "secret," and Sarvātma, the "Super-Soul." "The seven Lords of Being lie concealed in Sarvātma like thoughts in one brain." So are the Sephiroth. It is either seven when counting from the upper Triad headed by Kether, or ten — exoterically.
>
> — *SD* 1:89-90

In this connection the skull of 'Arīkh 'Anpīn with its seven conformations is comparable to the auric egg of the universe. More particularly, gŭlgaltā' may be described as the first unmanifest Logos, the highest of the three arūpa, nonmanifest worlds: the source and origin of all, to flower forth later in manifestation through Zĕ'ēir 'Anpīn.

There is a remarkable connection of thought between the quotation from *'Idrā' Rabbā'* (5:52), where the whiteness of the skull shines in thirteen sides — three portions of four sides each, and "in one above the skull, . . . the supernal side" — with the sections of chapter 2 of *'Idrā' Zūṭā'*, where gūlgaltā' is described as having no beginning, but whose end is the "convexity of its joining together," at which place the dew is distilled into Microprosopus, and from thence the dead are raised into life. This image parallels the teaching of the ancient mystical Hindus as well as of theosophy concerning the *Brahmarandhra*, defined as an "aperture in the crown of the head through which the soul is said to escape on its leaving the body" — a definition of occult significance.

This prominence on the skull where the dew is distilled into Microprosopus is one of the laya-centers or "zero points" between the two Faces ('anpīn), through which the supernal powers and energies of 'Arīkh 'Anpīn pass from the arūpa into the rūpa spheres of Zĕ'ēir 'Anpīn; in other words, to use a specific example, where the solar energies of the macrocosm pour into the microcosm (Zĕ'ēir 'Anpīn, our earth planetary chain) to manifest in physical form in Malkhūth (our physical earth).

Furthermore, the "thirteen carved out sides" divided into the three portions of four sides each, topped by the "one above the skull," are suggestive of the four great divisions of the universe symbolized by the Hindus as the four mahārājas (great kings) or the four lokapālas (world protectors), the four regents of the spaces resident at the four cardinal points: the north (the supernal side), south, east, and west. Again, these thirteen sides are comparable to the twelve zodiacal constellations, the thirteenth or supernal side being the laya-center or open doorway through which the "influences" (*mazzālōth*) from above may pass from the darkness of 'ēin sōf through Kether, and flowing through

'Arīkh 'Anpīn manifest in Zĕʿēir 'Anpīn, finding ultimate appearance in Malkhūth, our earth, as the twelve zodiacal influences.

The Dew: Second Conformation

'Idrā' Rabbā' states concerning the "dew or moisture of the brain of the Ancient One":

> And from that skull distilleth a dew upon Him which is external, and filleth His head daily (4:44).
>
> And from that dew which floweth down from his head, that (*namely*) which is external, the dead are raised up in the world to come (4:45).
>
> And by that dew are nourished the holy supernal ones (4:48).
>
> And that dew distilleth upon the ground of the holy apple trees. . . . (4:50).   — Mathers, pp. 116-17

Compare the above with a verse already quoted from 'Idrā' Zūṭā':

> And from this convexity of the joining together of this White Skull daily distilleth a dew into Microprosopus, into that place which is called Heaven; and in that very place shall the dead be raised to life in the time to come.
>
> — 2:53, Mathers, pp. 264-5

Ṭallā', the "dew" or "moisture," is the *svabhavat* of theosophic philosophy when viewed as identical with the second or manifest-unmanifest Logos. Purucker defines svabhavat as "the spiritual essence, the fundamental root or spirit-substance, the Father-Mother of the beginning of manifestation, and from it grow or *become* all things" (*Fundamentals*, p. 135).

Just as all things in nature merge into each other, so it is difficult to make a distinction between the first and second, and again between the second and third, conformations of 'Arīkh 'Anpīn. The first and second are most intimately connected, the one with the other. In theosophy, svabhavat is sometimes considered the equivalent of hiraṇyagarbha, and hence is called the first Logos; yet when viewed as the "highest ranges of ākāśa," svabhavat becomes the second Logos. In like manner, ṭallā' partakes of the attributes of both first and second Logoi as the link between the two, just as it is the link between the first conformation and the third, the "aetheric membrane" surrounding the concealed and tranquil brain. Or when considering the sĕfīrōth, ṭallā' as Ḥokhmāh is the link between Kether or the skull and Bīnāh or the aetheric membrane.

In HPB's *Theosophical Glossary*, ṭallā is described as the "fiery fluid of life and intelligence" distilled from the White Head "in three hundred and seventy streams, in all the directions of the Universe" (p. 277). This ṭallā' is not the ordinary dew of our earth, but the spiritual prototype of the earthly reflection: the phrase "fiery fluid" being HPB's way of suggesting the aetheric quality of spirit-substance, svabhavat, that condition of being where spirit and matter are one, where they are Father-Mother. Purucker describes this as

> a state or condition of kosmic consciousness-substance, where spirit and matter, which you know are *fundamentally* one, no longer are dual as in manifestation, but one: that which is neither manifested matter, nor manifested spirit, alone, but both are the primeval unity; spiritual ākāśa; where

matter merges into spirit, and both now being really one, are called Father-Mother, . . .

. . . the kalpic ākāśic spirit-substance, never descending from its own state or condition, or from its own plane, but the quasi-infinite reservoir of being, of consciousness, of light, of life, and the source of what science, in our day, so ridiculously calls the "forces" of nature universal.

. . . the Brahmanical scriptures call it ākāśa; and the Hebrew Old Testament refers to it as the kosmic "waters."

— *Fundamentals*, pp. 196-7

Likewise in *The Secret Doctrine* (2:400n), ākāśa is called the "fiery waters of space," indicating neither our terrestrial fire, nor our terrestrial water, but a primordial or arūpa condition.

The extracts from the *Zohar* are also connected with the mysteries of initiation where the disciple leaves the boundaries of the earth and partakes of the "manna of heaven . . . in the world to come." In this disguised language is found the age-old truth that the disciple of wisdom must "die" in the world of matter if he would be "raised up in the world to come," i.e., if he would be *reborn* as an adept, the "just," in the world of *spiritual forces*, svabhavat — that ṭallā' or dew which is distilled "in that place called heaven." "Heaven" — more correctly translated "heavens" — stands here for the invisible worlds of the spirit culminating in the central invisible Sun of the Qabbalist through whose portals "the holy supernal ones" may enter and receive the "holy apple trees," the fruits of spiritual wisdom "drawn upon at will at initiation" (*Esoteric Tradition* 2:1042).

In *The Mahatma Letters to A. P. Sinnett* svabhavat —

ṭallā', this world of force — is shown to be the world of occultism:

> The world of force is the world of Occultism and the only one whither the highest initiate goes to probe the secrets of being. Hence no-one but such an initiate can know anything of these secrets. Guided by his Guru the chela first discovers this world, then its laws, then their centrifugal evolutions into the world of matter. To become a perfect adept takes him long years, but at last he becomes the master. The hidden things have become patent, and mystery and miracle have fled from his sight forever. — Letter 22, pp. 143-4

The Aetheric Membrane: Third Conformation

Regarding the third conformation of the skull of 'Arīkh 'Anpīn, the aetheric membrane (*qĕrūmā' dĕ'awwēirā'*), 'Idrā' Rabbā' says:

> In the hollow of the skull is the aërial membrane of the supreme hidden Wisdom, which is nowhere disclosed; and it is not found, and it is not opened.
>
> And that membrane enshroudeth the brain [mōḥā'] of the hidden Wisdom [ḥokhmĕthā' sĕthīmā'āh], and therefore is that Wisdom covered, because it is not opened through that membrane.
>
> And that brain, which is itself the hidden Wisdom, is silent and remaineth tranquil in its place, like good wine upon its lees.
>
> And this is that which they say: — Hidden is the science of the Ancient One, and His brain is calm and concealed.
>
> And that membrane hath an outlet towards Microprosopus, and on that account is His brain extended, and goeth forth by thirty and two paths.
>
> — 6:58-62, Mathers, pp. 118-19

Qĕrūmā' dĕ'awwēirā' is translated by Mathers as "skin of ether" and as "aerial membrane"; and while both phrases are accurate enough, we prefer the equally correct translation of "membrane or film or veil of space or aether," or more concisely "aetheric membrane" — aetheric being a more inclusive term than aerial, and more suggestive of the philosophy imbodied in the term.

Qĕrūmā' dĕ'awwēirā', as the third conformation of the skull of the White Head, however, embraces not only this ākāśic film or aetheric membrane or covering, but likewise includes that which it enshrouds: the supreme hidden wisdom (ḥokhmĕthā' sĕthīmā'āh), called also the calm and concealed brain or the supernal brain (mōḥā' 'illā'āh). It is this aetheric membrane plus the hidden wisdom or concealed brain which corresponds to the third Logos, ākāśa proper. Note that the second conformation, dew, corresponds to the second Logos or svabhavat when viewed as the highest ranges of ākāśa, but that qĕrūmā' dĕ'awwēirā', produced from the first and second Logoi, is ākāśa in its totality.

Furthermore, the union of qĕrūmā' dĕ'awwēirā' with ḥokhmĕthā' sĕthīmā'āh corresponds to *mahat*, a Sanskrit term signifying the cosmic wisdom and intelligence or ideative power, the prototype or "Father-Mother" of the human mind, and the "mother" of the mānasaputras or "sons of mind" who enlightened humanity (*Fundamentals*, p. 406).

"And that membrane hath an outlet towards Microprosopus, and on that account is His brain extended": here we have the third Logos becoming the progenitor in its turn of the innumerable minor Logoi which form Zĕ'ēir 'Anpīn. This is comparable to the theosophical teaching of the mānasaputras — the lightbringers, "sons of mind" — those divinely equipped beings whose work is the lighting of the fires of intelligence and wisdom in infant humanity.

The Hair: Fourth Conformation

The fourth conformation of the skull of 'Arīkh 'Anpīn is called "hair" (*nīmā'*), of which *'Idrā' Rabbā'* states:

> This is the tradition. From the skull of His head hang down a thousand thousand myriads; seven thousand and five hundred curling hairs, white and pure, like as wool when it is pure; which have not been mingled confusedly together lest inordinate disorder should be shown in His conformation; but all are in order, so that no one lock may go beyond another lock, nor one hair before another (7:65).
>
> But these hairs, all and singular, radiate into four hundred and ten worlds (7:67).
>
> And He radiateth in seven hundred and twenty directions (*others say four hundred and twenty*).
>
> And in all the hairs is a fountain, which issueth from the hidden brain behind the wall of the skull.
>
> And it shineth and goeth forth through that hair unto the hair of Microprosopus, and from it is His brain formed; and thence that brain goeth forth into thirty and two paths (7:69-71).
>
> But the curls of the hair are disposed on each side of the skull.
>
> Also we have said: Each hair is said to be the breaking of the hidden fountains, issuing from the concealed brain (7:73-4).   — Mathers, pp. 119-20

'Idrā' Zūṭā' states:

But all those hairs and all those locks depend from the Hidden Brain (2:66).

One (*path*) which shineth in the midst of the hairs going forth from the Skull, is that path by whose light the just are led into the world to come.

Like as it is written, Prov. iv, 18: "And the path of the just shineth as the light" (2:70-71).

And from that path are all the other paths illuminated which depend from Microprosopus (2:73).

— Mathers, pp. 266-7

Nīmā', the hair which hangs down from the skull of 'Arīkh 'Anpīn in myriads of curling hairs, "white and pure," unconfused and orderly, suggests the hosts of monadic lives in their arūpa (bodiless) condition before they become heavy with matter, confused and mingled in the rūpa (body) worlds. They are the noumena or cause of what later will be phenomena in Zě'ēir 'Anpīn, as the series of life-waves or hosts of monads become then locks of "black hair," intertwined and mingled, where "pure and impure alike adhere to each other therein," as *'Idrā' Rabbā'* describes it.

"And in all the hairs is a fountain" — that is, in each entity of the armies of life-waves there resides the hidden monadic fire, the inextinguishable spark of eternity which "issueth from the hidden brain," i.e., which springs forth from the third Logos (mahat, cosmic ideation).

There is here a suggestion of various types of monadic hosts, first "into thirty and two paths" and again "on each side of the skull," signifying what later will become bipolarity in manifestation. But most significant is the section describing the "one path which shineth in the midst of the hairs going forth from the skull, . . . that path by whose light the just are led into the world to come."

The Forehead: Fifth Conformation

'Idrā' Rabbā' describes the fifth conformation, the forehead (*mitsḥā'*), in the following manner:

> And that forehead is called RTzVN [*Rātsōn*], Will-power, because it is the ruler of the whole head and of the skull, which is covered by four hundred and twenty worlds (8:90).
>
> This is the tradition: This forehead hath been extended into two hundred and seventy thousand lights of the luminaries of the superior Eden (8:105).
>
> The inferior Eden is distributed into its paths; (*namely*) into thirty-two directions of its paths.
>
> And although this Eden is distributed into its path, yet is it not known unto any, save unto Microprosopus.
>
> But no man hath known the superior Eden, nor its paths, except Macroprosopus Himself (8:107-9).
>
> "The Elohim understand the way thereof:" this is the inferior Eden, known unto Microprosopus. "And He hath known the place thereof:" this is the superior Eden, which the Ancient of Days hath known, the most abstruse of all (8:111).   — Mathers, pp. 122-4

In *'Idrā' Zūṭā'* it is written:

> And when this Head, which is concealed in the Head of the Ancient One, which is not known, extendeth a certain frontal formation, which is formed for brilliance, then flasheth forth the Lightning of His Brain.
>
> And it is formed forth and illuminated with many Lights.
>   — 3:108-9, Mathers, p. 270

Note the theosophical parallels suggested here: the forehead of 'Arīkh 'Anpīn, described as *rātsōn*, the fire of will combined with grace or compassion, suggests the ancient conception of universes coming into being partly through will and karma, and partly through love or compassion; and the 420 worlds and the 270,000 lights extending from mitshā' are those luminous seeds of spirit which, given the appropriate time and space, issue from the divine intelligence as universes, whether stars, atoms, or human beings.

The superior Eden comprehended only by Kether, the Macroprosopus, the Crown of the sĕfīrōth, symbolizes the upper arūpa worlds, the unmanifest spheres — Kether or 'Arīkh 'Anpīn standing as the guardian between our hierarchy and the one above, the open doorway receiving the light from above and transmitting it to all the smaller lights below, represented here by the 'elohīm or various classes of angels or dhyāni-chohans comprised in Zĕ'ēir 'Anpīn, who "know the way" of the inferior Eden, the rūpa or manifested worlds.

The "frontal formation" which flashes forth the lightning of the brain of 'Arīkh 'Anpīn is the fire of mahat (divine mind) which, descending from the superior arūpa worlds, becomes in the rūpa worlds of Zĕ'ēir 'Anpīn, the mānasaputric fire which illumines the lower sĕfīrōth.

The Open Eye: Sixth Conformation

The open eye ('*ēinā' pĕqīḥā'*) is given as the sixth conformation in the skull of 'Arīkh 'Anpīn. As '*Idrā' Rabbā'* states:

The eyes of the White Head are diverse from all other

eyes. Above the eye is no eyelid, neither is there an eyebrow over it (9:112).

And this is the tradition: This eye is never closed; and there are two, and they are converted into one.

All is right; there is no left there. He sleepeth not and slumbereth not, and He requireth not protection. He is not such an one as hath need to defend Himself, for He defendeth all things, and He Himself waited upon all things, and in the sight of His eye are all things established.

This is the tradition: Were that eye closed even for one moment, no thing could subsist.

Therefore is it called the open eye, the holy eye, the excellent eye, the eye of Providence,* the eye which sleepeth not neither slumbereth, the eye which is the guardian of all things, the eye which is the subsistence of all things (9:134-7).

And to no man is it known when this superior holy eye may shine and may bathe the inferior; and when the just and the supernal blessed ones are about to be beheld in that Wisdom (9:140).

And unless the bountiful superior eye were to look down upon and bathe the inferior eye, the universe could not exist even a single moment (9:142).

. . . In the eyes which are inferior are a right eye and a left eye, and they are of two diverse colours.

But in this instance there is no left eye, and they both ascend in one path, and all are right. And on that account is one eye mentioned, and not two.

And this is the tradition: This eye, which is the eye of observation, is ever open, ever smiling, ever glad.

---

*In Aramaic and Hebrew: 'ēinā' pĕqīḥā'; 'ēinā' 'illā'āh; 'ēinā' qaddīshā'; 'ēinā' dĕ-'ashgāḥūthā'.

Such are not the inferiors, who in themselves have red-
ness, and blackness, and whiteness — three colours; and are
not always open, for there are eyelids as a protection over
these eyes (9:149-52).   — Mathers, pp. 124, 127-9

The open eye of 'Arīkh 'Anpīn, where bipolarity does not
exist and which needs no protection or eyelid, which is ever
smiling and glad (compassionate), which defends not itself
but is the defender and champion of all, is reminiscent of
the Silent Watcher of our hierarchy — the prototype and
source of the Mahāguru of our earth, called by HPB the
supreme sacrifice, the great Being

who changes form, yet remains ever the same. And it is
he again who holds spiritual sway over the *initiated* Adepts
throughout the whole world. He is, as said, the "Name-
less One" who has so many names, and yet whose names
and whose very nature are unknown. He is *the* "Initiator,"
called the "GREAT SACRIFICE." For, sitting at the threshold of
LIGHT, he looks into it from within the circle of Darkness,
which he will not cross; nor will he quit his post till the last
day of this life-cycle. Why does the solitary Watcher remain
at his self-chosen post? Why does he sit by the fountain of
primeval Wisdom, of which he drinks no longer, as he has
naught to learn which he does not know — aye, neither on
this Earth, nor in its heaven? Because the lonely, sore-footed
pilgrims on their way back to their *home* are never sure to the
last moment of not losing their way in this limitless desert
of illusion and matter called Earth-Life. Because he would
fain show the way to that region of freedom and light, from
which he is a voluntary exile himself, to every prisoner who
has succeeded in liberating himself from the bonds of flesh
and illusion. Because, in short, he has sacrificed himself for

the sake of mankind, though but a few Elect may profit by
the GREAT SACRIFICE. — *SD* 1:207-8

That the "Universe could not exist even a single moment" were the "bountiful superior eye" to refuse to "bathe
the inferior eye" means that all things that exist on this
earth could not possibly do so unless such manifestation
and appearances were continuously "bathed" by the boundless light of spirit emanating from the open eye of the arūpa
worlds of 'Arīkh 'Anpīn. In other words, matter is nonex-
istent except as the other pole of spirit. Again *'Idrā' Rabbā'*
says:

> Rabbi Schimeon spake unto Rabbi Abba, and said: "To
> what is this [the Open Eye] like?" He answered unto him:
> "To the whales and fishes of the sea, which have no coverings
> for their eyes, nor eyebrows above their eyes; who sleep not,
> and require not a protection for the eye.
>
> "How much less doth the Ancient of the Ancient Ones
> require a protection, seeing that He far above His creatures
> watcheth over all things, and all things are nourished by
> Him, and He Himself sleepeth not."
>
> — 9:116-17, Mathers, p. 125

This one eye, the open eye of 'Arīkh 'Anpīn, becomes in
Zĕ'ēir 'Anpīn the two eyes of spirit and matter, the eyes
needing protection, the eyes that require sleep, but which,
according to HPB, will in the future become one.

The Nose or Nostrils: Seventh Conformation

Ḥōṭāmā', the seventh and last conformation as given in
the Mantuan Codex, is described in *'Idrā' Rabbā'*:

> This nose is as a mighty gallery, whence His Spirit rusheth forth upon Microprosopus, and they call it the Giver. And it is thus: The Spirit descendeth; and again the Spirit from hence proceedeth through those nostrils (10:175-6). And from that gallery ariseth the Spirit, and proceedeth from the concealed brain, and at length resteth upon King Messiah (10:179). — Mathers, p. 131

In *'Idrā' Zūṭā'* it is written:

> For the nose of Him, the Ancient One, is the life of lives for all things, and from His two nostrils rush forth the RVChIN DChIIN [*Rūḥīn děḤayyīn*], spirits of lives for all (15:561).
>
> ... From this nose, from the openings of the nostrils, the Spirit of Life rusheth forth upon Microprosopus (5:136).
>
> And that Spirit proceedeth from the hidden brain, and She is called the Spirit of Life, and through that Spirit will all men understand ChKMThA [*Ḥokhměthā'*] Wisdom, in the time of King Messiah (5:138). — Mathers, pp. 316, 273

The rushing rivers of lives of this seventh conformation of the skull of 'Arīkh 'Anpīn are those seeds of spirit, of cosmic mind, or as the Stoics expressed it, the spermatikoi logoi (seeds of the Logoi) which "proceedeth from the concealed brain" (mōḥā' 'illā'āh), later to pour through the beard (dīqnā') of 'Arīkh 'Anpīn into Zě'ēir 'Anpīn, there to become the life-waves of the manifested worlds.

The phrase *rūḥīn děḤayyīn* is significant: *rūḥīn* (plural of *rūaḥ*), "spirits, winds, breaths," not bodies or forms, but the spiritual essences which in their own time and space in Zě'ēir 'Anpīn or the rūpa worlds will become the living beings, the seven, ten, or twelve life-waves of theosophy.

In this symbolism, 'Arīkh 'Anpīn has been correlated to the arūpa worlds of ideation, in which are selected and prepared the germs or seeds of future worlds and living hosts which will manifest in Zĕ'ēir 'Anpīn. The conformations of the skull which comprise 'Arīkh 'Anpīn are given as seven in number, but they might have been given as three or five. Theosophy generally refers to five unmanifest and seven manifest worlds, though references are made to seven unmanifest as the prototype or Father-Mother of the manifest seven; again, three arūpa worlds are at times held to contain the spiritual seeds of life to germinate and fructify on the seven rūpa planes.

Describing these seven supernal conformations as specifically allocated in the Mantuan Codex, does not mean that all Qabbalistic writers give this numeration to each conformation of the skull, i.e., that the hair is always the fourth, or that the open eye must necessarily be the sixth. But the conformations, regardless of specific numbering, are described in a consistent manner in three important books of the *Zohar*, reiterating the age-old truth that all things later to flower on and in the manifested worlds issue first as seeds of spirit in the unmanifest.

Thus what might appear as needless repetition is no such thing; it is, rather, a remarkably effective manner of stating this truth. To illustrate: the first three conformations of 'Arīkh 'Anpīn are, as stated earlier, correlated to the first, second, and third Logoi; in Zĕ'ēir 'Anpīn they will again be described as the first three Logoi — not as mere repetition, but precisely because the three Logoi allocated to Macroprosopus are the prototype, the Father-Mother,

of the three Logoi of Microprosopus. The remaining four
conformations of the White Head again demonstrate how
the seeds of that which is to be, are prepared in 'Arīkh 'Anpīn for germination and flowering in the manifested worlds
of Zĕ'ēir 'Anpīn. The implication is that nothing could
exist or appear in Zĕ'ēir 'Anpīn were it not for sowing of
the seed in 'Arīkh 'Anpīn. Hence all lives — whether stars,
men, beasts, or the stones underneath our feet — are spirits, *rūḥīn*, vital breaths, and not mere forms or bodies, and
these *rūḥīn dĕḤayyīn* are united in Kether or 'Arīkh 'Anpīn,
in the self universal, paramātman.

The Beard: Link between
Macroprosopus and Microprosopus

From these seven conformations of 'Arīkh 'Anpīn hangs
the Beard (*dīqnā'*), called the "beard of truth" (*dīqnā' di-
mĕḥēimĕnūthā'*), also the "dignity of dignities," and described therein as "white as snow" in contrast to the inferior
beard of Zĕ'ēir 'Anpīn, "black and bushy as the raven."

From the cranium of the White Head the Beard depends
in four and nine conformations, the upper four pertaining
to Macroprosopus, while the lower nine "flow upon the
body" of Microprosopus. Again, it is through dīqnā' that
the concealed power of 'Arīkh 'Anpīn or the superior worlds
is most abundantly transferred as through a laya-center to
its reflection Zĕ'ēir 'Anpīn; for through each of these thirteen conformations a holy influence (*mazzālā' qaddīshā'*)
flows, from which influence stream thirteen "fountains of
precious oil" — a most suggestive inclusion here, for the
word oil (*mishḥā'*) symbolizes initiation and all that this

word implies. The word Messiah is the anglicized form of the Hebrew *Māshīah,* meaning "anointed," one upon and through whom the "fountain of precious oil" has flowed from the superior worlds of his own inner being, as well as surrounding nature, and thus "anointed" or initiated him.

In the following extracts from the *Zohar,* this "oil of magnificence" (*mishhā' di-rĕbūthā'*) is significant, for it is the bearer of the holy influence from 'Arīkh 'Anpīn, the supernal worlds, to Zĕ'eir 'Anpīn, and from the latter into Maṭrōnīthā', his Bride or Shĕkhīnāh, the dwelling place or receiver of the tenfold powers of the tree of lives. Interpreting this as symbolic of the sanctuary, this holy influence (*mazzālā' qaddīshā',* which may also be translated the "holy stars or planets") could signify the spiritual solar power that emanates from our own star, the sun: both universally in the life-giving impulses that constantly rejuvenate; and specifically in those sun-men — avatāras, christs, buddhas, and the like. These "anointed" ones come forth from the interior chambers of the sun to appear at periodic intervals to liberate the spirits in chains by pouring their "precious balm," their "oil of greatness," upon those worthy to receive the *Sōd* or mysteries.

The *Sifrā' di-Tsĕnī'ūthā'* states:

> Of the beard mention hath not been made. Because this is the ornament of all. . . .
>
> . . . Into thirteen portions it is distributed in adornment (2:2-3).

Through thirteen springs are the fountains distributed (by which there is an influx upon Microprosopus and the inferiors). Four are separately joined together, but nine flow upon the body, encircle the garden (that is, the Microprosopus) (2:5).

In that influence of all stream down thirteen drops of most pure balm.

In this influence all things exist and are concealed (2:17-18). — Mathers, pp. 66-8

In *'Idrā' Rabbā'*, dīqnā' is more elaborately treated:

Through those thirteen dispositions do they flow down, and the thirteen fountains of precious oil issue forth, and they flow down through all those inferiors, and in that oil do they shine, and with that oil are they anointed (11:229).

— Mathers, p. 136

Therefore is it said that (in Macroprosopus) all the hairs descend equally from the head and beard; for the hair of the head is prolonged even unto the shoulders, so that it may reach unto the head of Microprosopus, from that flux of the one brain unto the other (11:242).

Since there is not subsistence in the inferior brain except by the preservation of the supernal brain (11:246).

— Mathers, p. 138

Who can comprehend the mystery of those locks of hair which hang down from Him, the Ancient One?

He is set on the crown of crowns, which are the crowns of all crowns, and the crowns which are not comprehended in the other crowns; I say, of those crowns which are not as the other crowns, for the inferior crowns are comprehended by them [i.e., the sĕfīrōth].

And therefore are those forms (arranged in) such conformations, whereunto the inferior forms adhere; . . . (12:309-311).

We have learned: Unless the Ancient of the Ancient

Ones, the Holy of the Holy Ones, were disposed in those conformations, neither the superiors nor the inferiors would be found, and all things would be as though they existed not.

Also we have learned by tradition: how far do those conformations of the beard radiate splendour? Even unto the thirteen inferiors; and whensoever those thirteen are found, those shine (12:314-15).   — Mathers, pp. 144-5

And all the concealed superiors and inferiors are concealed in it, and they are comprehended in that Influx from which all things emanate; like as it is said:

And that day is not comprehended in them, seeing it comprehendeth all things (23:475-6).

For thus we have learned. In that place where there is day there is also night, seeing that day cannot exist without night (23:480).

It is called neither day nor night, for it is not called day except for our (*better understanding of the symbolism involved*), neither is it called night except for the same reason.

And because that form includeth all things, hence nothing whatsoever is known or seen concerning it.

And from it streameth down the oil of magnificence in thirteen directions, which flow down upon all the inferiors in order that they may shine forth.

In that oil are consummated the thirteen parts of the holy and excellent beard.

And those forms which are in that beard are disposed and descend in many directions, neither can it be seen how they are extended nor how they arise.

They are hidden in all things, and they are concealed in all things; and no man knoweth their place, except Him, the Ancient One (23:482-7).   — Mathers, pp. 167-8

10

The Fourfold Nature of Man

Lɪᴋᴇ ᴍᴏsᴛ ᴀɴᴄɪᴇɴᴛ ᴘᴇᴏᴘʟᴇs, the Hebrews saw man as a copy of the universe. He thus contains all the potencies thereof: spiritual, vital, material. Hence, Qabbalistic philosophy pictures each human being as comprising a number of elements:

> when the Holy One created man He took the dust of the lower Sanctuary, but for the making of his soul He chose the dust of the upper Sanctuary. Just as in the formation of man's body from the dust of the lower Sanctuary, three cosmic elements [air, fire, water] were combined, so in the formation of his soul from the dust of the upper Sanctuary, further elements, to the number of three, were mingled, and so man was completely formed.
>
> — *Zohar* 3:24b, Sperling 3:82

Generally, Qabbālāh divides the human constitution into four aspects. The highest element is *nĕshāmāh*, meaning "breath, spirit, wind." This spirit or divine breath is equivalent to the *pneuma* of the Greeks (from *pneō*, "to breathe"), the Latin *spiritus* (from *spiro*, "to breathe"), and the Sanskrit *ātman* (from *an*, "to blow, to breathe"). Nĕshāmāh is the essential consciousness, the first "breath" from 'ēin sōf, which animates the rest of the human being. Sometimes it has been mistaken for the vital principle in the human body (ḥai) because it is spoken of as the breath of God. The vital essence of the lower part of the human constitution is the reflection of nĕshāmāh, much as in theosophy the prāṇas are the representation on the lower planes of ātma-buddhi in the human being. After death nĕshāmāh "goes up direct to the very inner" (*Zohar* 2:142a, Myer, p. 394).

The second element is *rūaḥ*, also "breath," the spiritual soul. It is comparable to the Greek *nous*, the Latin *mens*, and to buddhi-manas or spiritual soul. It is ruled by and forms the throne or vehicle of nĕshāmāh. In connection with 'elohīm, rūaḥ denotes the mental quality of the gods, regarded in *Genesis* as moving over the waters of space or chaos at creation. Equivalent to the third Logos, it operates through the universe, producing what is noble and good in human beings and leading them to virtue. A similar meaning implies exceptional soul powers, as in the inspired ruler or prophet, hence the prophetic spirit, often represented as passing from one person to another. After death the rūaḥ goes up to Eden, but not so high as the nĕshāmāh.

The third element is *nefesh*, the "vital breath" or lower human soul. It corresponds to the *psuchē* of the Greeks, the Latin *anima*, and modern theosophy's lower mind — kāma-prāṇa with the breath of manas (mind) upon it. Being closely associated with the physical body, it has no light of its own. It is the throne of rūaḥ which rules and lights it and forms its crown. After death the nefesh or lower soul "remains in the grave Below" (ibid.).

These three breaths find expression on earth in *gūf*, the physical body, which corresponds to the sthūla-śarīra, the Latin *corpus*, and the Greek *sōma*. It is significant that the first three aspects — nĕshāmāh, rūaḥ, and nefesh — should all be derived from words meaning "breath" or "wind." The Qabbalist understood the esoteric lining of truth, for all are manifestations in degree of the one fundamental breath of Being: nĕshāmāh, the breath of divinity; rūaḥ, the breath of spiritual mentation; and nefesh, the breath of psychic vitality. These three breaths each has its field of action in one of the three higher 'ōlāmīm above the fourth world of qĕlīppōth or shells, where gūf is at home. Each is sustained by the element above it.

> From observing these grades of the soul, one obtains an insight into the higher Wisdom, and it is wholly through Wisdom that in this way certain mysteries are connected together. — *Zohar* 1:83b, Sperling 1:278

Nĕshāmāh, rūaḥ, and nefesh may be looked at in several ways. Nefesh and rūaḥ are sometimes seen as two aspects of one grade, and when nĕshāmāh

> enters into them and they cleave to it, and when it dominates, such a man is called holy, perfect, wholly devoted to God. "Soul" (*nefesh*) is the lowest stirring, it supports and feeds the body and is closely connected with it. When it sufficiently qualifies itself, it becomes the throne on which rests the lower spirit (*ruaḥ*), . . . When both have prepared themselves sufficiently, they are qualified to receive the higher spirit (*neshamah*), to which the lower spirit (*ruaḥ*) becomes a throne, and which is undiscoverable, supreme over all. — Ibid.

Using the analogy of the flame, nefesh is likened to the blue light at the bottom of the flame, which is attached to and exists through the wick (gūf).

When fully kindled it becomes a throne for the white light above it. When both are fully kindled, the white light becomes a throne for a light which cannot be fully discerned, an unknown something resting on that white light, and so there is formed a complete light.　　　　— Ibid.

When we are born we are endowed with nefesh "from the primordial 'animal' sphere, the sphere of purity, . . . the supernal order of angels," also referred to as the perennial celestial stream. When we achieve purity in this aspect, we will be endowed with rūaḥ "which appertains to the sphere of the Holy *Hayoth* [living beings]." Rūaḥ forms a crown to nefesh. These two principles are intertwined, and if we do not strive after spiritual things, that is the extent of our being. But those of greater merit are endowed with nĕshāmāh "from the region of the Throne" (*Zohar* 3:94b, Sperling 3:283-4). The nĕshāmāh descends to the nefesh and rūaḥ, so that all three combine harmoniously to form a unity in those who serve the Divine:

> the *neshamah* resides in a man's character — an abode which cannot be discovered or located. Should a man strive towards purity of life, he is aided thereto by a holy *neshamah*, whereby he is purified and sanctified . . .
> 　　　　　　　　　　　— *Zohar* 1:62a, Sperling 1:203

Over the body and the three souls is a fourth, supernal soul, which is

inscrutable and unknowable. Everything is dependent upon

it, and it is veiled in a covering of exceeding brightness. It drops pearls which are linked together like the joints of the body, and it enters into them and displays through them its energy. It and they are one, and there is no separation between them. — *Zohar* 2:245a, Sperling 2:378-9

Sometimes the highest principle "which remains above" is called the *tsūrāh* or divine "prototypal form." This tsūrāh is equivalent to the spiritual monad. It produces the něshāmāh as its reflection, and they are connected by a vital spiritual thread up which the něshāmāh aspires to rise to perfect union with its prototype. Another term for this highest part of the human being is *yěḥīdāh* (the one, the only, the unique), the indivisible individuality of the human constitution. This term is comparable to the Greek word *monas*, meaning "one."

A further aspect of manifested beings is brought out in this striking statement:

Over all these stars and constellations of the firmament there have been set chiefs, leaders, and ministers, whose duty is to serve the world each one according to his appointed station. And not the tiniest grass-blade on earth but has its own appointed star in heaven. Each star, too, has over it a being appointed who ministers before the Holy One as its representative, each according to his order. All the stars in the firmaments keep watch over this world: they are appointed to minister to every individual object in this world, to each object a star. Herbs and trees, grass and wild plants, cannot flourish and grow except from the influence of the stars who stand above them and gaze upon them face to face, each according to his fashion. — *Zohar* 4:171b, Sperling 4:92-3

The doctrine of reincarnation appears in the *Zohar* as the teaching of *gilgūlīm* (wheels), the revolution of souls, but it is more implied than explicit. Also implied is the idea that everything exists in divine form before birth. Qabbalists hold that the soul after death goes through a series of whirlings, which apply both to the transmigration of the physical and other atoms, and to the reimbodiment of souls (cf. *SD* 1:568n).

The soul puts on garments appropriate to the sphere which it is to enter. Before birth it wears cloaks of higher light ('ōr). All is hidden in the divine form before it takes birth; hence the soul is the expression of its past karma within its divine form. All the forms of the earthly world were originally fashioned of supernal light in the Garden of Eden, the habitation of holy spirits.

After birth, while in gūf, the soul wears a cloak of skin or blindness ('ōr). At death the soul removes the lower cloak of blindness and ascends into the inner worlds. The body has returned to dust and the soul is clothed in luminous garments. The nefesh disintegrates with the body, the rūaḥ stays in the Garden of Eden, and the něshāmāh "ascends to the place where all delights are concentrated" (*Zohar* 2:226a-b, Sperling 2:326). When it leaves the Garden to imbody, the soul takes off its celestial garment and puts on an earthly body. Then when it leaves the earth, the Angel of Death takes off the earthly body so it can again put on the celestial garments in the Garden of Eden that it had left behind there.

There are two lines of human evolution: (1) recession of spiritual capacity as "cloaks of higher light" ('ōr, אוֹר) become veiled through material descent; and (2) the expansion of a physical "cloak of blindness," of matter ('ōr, עוֹר).

Adam then arose and realised that he was both of heaven and of earth, and so he united himself to the Divine and was endowed with mystic Wisdom. Each son of man is, after the same model, a composite of the heavenly and the earthly. — *Zohar* 2:130b, Sperling 2:20

11

Sleep, Death, and Initiation

Něshāmāh, rūaḥ, and nefesh each has its own function in waking, in sleep and dreams, and after death. In sleep and dreams něshāmāh and rūaḥ travel upwards or downwards according to the quality of the waking consciousness — our aspiration or lack of it. When we sleep, our nefesh leaves the body and "tries to soar from grade to grade," encountering "bright but unclean essences." If undefiled during the day, it rises above them; if not, "it becomes defiled among them and cleaves to them and does not rise any further." These unclean essences show the nefesh things which will happen in the near future, and "sometimes they delude her and show her false things. Thus she goes about the whole night until the man wakes up, when she returns to her place" (*Zohar* 1:83a, Sperling 1:277). The soul of one undefiled during the day is not enticed by false powers, but continues to ascend further, and finally comes to the gate of the celestial palace, and seeks out "the holy essence in the place from which she (originally) issued" (ibid.).

Thus the journey of the soul in sleep depends on each person's deeds and attachments. The Supreme Point or Kether "absorbs in itself the souls of the righteous." The holy angels then communicate to it true information which the soul on its return communicates to the person through dreams or visions. When the soul descends again, the evil powers are eager to obtain from it this divine information, offering to impart many other things in exchange. But their information is much inferior. Thus people have the dreams that answer to their grade of consciousness and action:

> dreams are under the charge of a hierarchy of custodians, so that some dreams are altogether true and others are a mixture of true and false. But to the truly righteous no false messages are ever communicated, but all they are told is true. . . . The unjust man is thus shown a happy dream, but an untruthful one, so as to make him go further astray from the path of truth. For since he turned aside from the right path they defile him the more, as whoever sets out to purify himself is purified from above, and whoever sets out to defile himself is similarly defiled from above.
>
> — *Zohar* 2:199b, 200a, Sperling 2:258, 259-60

Just as the Greeks held that sleep and death are brothers, so likewise the Hebrews:

> Similar adventures await the souls when they altogether leave the body to depart from this world. In their attempt to soar upwards they have to pass through many gates at which bands of demons are stationed. . . . On the other hand, the worthy souls soar upwards, as already explained, and are assigned the places corresponding to their merits.
>
> — *Zohar* 2:130a-b, Sperling 2:19

Thirty days before death, Dūmāh, Angel of Death, intimates to the nĕshāmāh its future, and something leaves the person: tsūlmā' (Hebrew tselem), "shadow, image, shade."

R. Jose said: "When a man's appointed time draws near, proclamation is made concerning him for thirty days, and even the birds of the heaven announce his doom; and if he is virtuous, his coming is announced for thirty days among the righteous in the Garden of Eden. We have learnt that during those thirty days his soul departs from him every night and ascends to the other world and sees its place there, and during those thirty days the man has not the same consciousness or control of his soul as previously." R. Judah said: "From the first arrival of those thirty days a man's shadow becomes faint and his form is not outlined clearly on the ground."

— *Zohar* 2:217b, Sperling 2:306

When death is near, "a new spirit enters into him from above, in virtue of which he sees things which he could not see before, and then he departs from the world" (*Zohar* 2:218b, Sperling 2:309). At death "all the days that he has lived in this world pass in review before Him" (*Zohar* 2:221b, Sperling 2:313). Three messengers or angels stand over the dying, taking down an account of all that he has done with his body and spirit while alive. He "admits all with his mouth and signs the account with his hand, . . . so that he should be judged in the next world for all his actions" (*Zohar* 1:79a, Sperling 1:266). Nothing is lost or forgotten:

In the centre of the heaven there is an illumined path, which is the celestial dragon, and in it are fixed multitudes of little stars which are charged to keep watch over the secret deeds of human beings. In the same way myriads of emissaries go forth from the primeval celestial serpent, by whom Adam was seduced, to spy out the secret deeds of mankind. Whoever, therefore, strives to live a life of purity is assisted from on high, and is encircled by the protecting hand of his Master, and is called saintly. On the other hand, when a man seeks to pollute himself, hosts of demons, who lie in wait for him, hover over him and surround and pollute him, so that he is called unclean. — *Zohar* 2:125a-b, Sperling 2:10

Every day in which our good prompter is sovereign is a good day gained after death, and every day that the evil prompter dominates is a bad day, a day lost after death. After death our days are counted, and there must be at least a majority of good days in order to ascend into the upper spheres. The vesture in which the soul appears before the Almighty is formed of these days and is glorious or the reverse according to the quality of each day of the life on earth. Those days spoiled by sins are missing and make the vesture defective. If there are many missing, the soul has no clothes in the other world. Further, it is punished in Gehenna many days for each missing day.

Because karma or exact balance must forever be established, each person goes after death whither he is attracted, "since the grades assigned to souls in the next world correspond to their state on departing from this world" (*Zohar* 2:193a, Sperling 2:235-6). This may be the Upper Eden, the Inferior Eden, or Gehenna, according to his deserts. There is no Savior for us except our good deeds, which are our only defense after death: "The righteous is judged by the good impulse, the sinner by the evil impulse, and the intermediate, he who is between these two extremes, is judged by both" (*Zohar* 3:41b, Sperling 3:127). Every word we speak causes a vibration in the higher spheres, and becomes an entity to plague or bless us.

First the departed must go to the sphere below the lowest ʿōlām: the land of Shĕʾōl. This realm corresponds to the Greek Hades or Orcus, a place where the shades or astral remnants of human beings remain after death to dissipate. There are ten degrees of ever more material density until the lowest hells are reached where only the utterly depraved find lodgment. In the Old Testament, Shĕʾōl is generally translated "hell" or "the pit." It is the abode both of the righteous and the unrighteous, where life is continued as a shadowy, wavering reflection of earth life. Souls there have no part in earth life nor is there any knowledge or productive work there (*Eccl* 9). While Shĕʾōl is a region of inactivity and stillness, Gehenna is both the region and the state of active dissolution of the compounded nefesh, the astral remains or kāma-rūpas bereft of their higher principles.

The purgatorial state of Gehenna has "seven circuits and seven gates, each with several gate-keepers under their own chief" (*Zohar* 2:237b, Sperling 2:357). There are seven habitations for the seven types of sinners, and thousands of angels under the Angel of Death punish the souls there.

> When the man comes near his time to go away from this world, . . . when the herald calls out (the decree), at once, a flame comes forth from the North side and goes in and ignites the river *Dinur* [*nĕhar dī-nūr*], (*i.e.*, the river of fire, comp. Dan. vii, 10) and spreads itself out to four sides of the world and burns the souls of the guilty, and that flame goes forth and comes down on the world . . .
>
> — *Zohar* 1:218b, Myer, p.405

The *Zohar* states further that "The fire of the Gehenna

which is below comes from the Gehenna which is above, and is kindled by the heat of the sinners in whom the evil inclination burns, . . ." In Gehenna the souls polluted by the "filth of this world" are "purified by fire and made white, and then they ascend towards the heavenly regions" (*Zohar* 4:150b, Sperling 4:28). Their impurities remain below, ruled over by the fire of Gehenna.

Those who sin repeatedly without repenting, who never turned to their Lord and have caused others to sin, remain in the earthly Gehenna or Shě'ōl forever (*Zohar* 4:151a; Sperling 4:29). The souls of those who intended to repent "flutter upward" after a time of purgation:

> The most wicked sinner, if he have intended repentance, but dies without carrying out his resolve, is, it is true, punished for having gone out of this world without having repented, but his good intention is not lost, but it ascends to the Supernal King and there remains until the Holy One, seeing it, prepares for that soul a place of refuge in "Sheol," where it twitters repentance. — *Zohar* 4:150a; Sperling 4:26-7

The good intention, issuing from God, breaks through all the gates of Gehenna to smite the soul and re-awaken the intention to repent. The soul then struggles to ascend from Shě'ōl. Those who repent and feel remorse are forgiven, but those who "cling to their sins and refuse to repent of them will in the end descend to Gehinnom and never come up again" (*Zohar* 1:66a, Sperling 1:218).

After being purified in Shě'ōl and Gehenna, the soul may clothe itself in the garments of its good thoughts and deeds which are garments of the higher light. It enters the lower Garden of Eden, which exactly reflects its prototype, the upper Paradise. Here the soul

> rests and moves, and contemplates continually the supernal mysteries which, when he was in the earthly body, he could neither grasp nor understand. When the soul clothes herself with the garments of that world, what delights, what joys, she experiences! And who caused the body to be inhabited by the spirit? Why, he who took off the garment of flesh, the Angel of Death! — *Zohar* 4:150a, Sperling 4:26

Stories of a Paradise or Eden are universal, both as the state of innocence and bliss from which humanity departs and to which it eventually will return, either individually after death or as a whole after the course of earthly evolution is completed. The Eden of *Genesis* is a compression of many aspects, just as the several Adams are presented as one individual in the Bible. Eden (delight) is thought to be an ancient name for Mesopotamia and adjacent regions, a sacred land from which human races emerged, and a goal of bliss in the future. These Edens or Paradises contain trees which signify the tree of life or lives and the tree of wisdom or knowledge. Eden may also signify initiation into spiritual knowledge.

A river known only to the initiated flows from the Lower Eden. Souls coming from earth thirst for the light of the Garden and rest by this river in their ethereal garments, without which they could not endure the celestial light:

> but protected by this covering they are in comfort and drink their fill of that radiance without being overwhelmed by it. It is the river which renders the souls fit and able to

feast on and to enjoy that radiance. The celestial river brings forth the souls who fly off into the Garden; the lower river in the terrestrial Garden, on the other hand, builds up the souls and makes them fit and able to enjoy those radiances, and so to mount up to the celestial Paradise through the central opening of the firmament and by the pillar that stands in the centre of the Lower Paradise. That pillar is enveloped in cloud and smoke and bright flashes, the cloud and smoke encircling it from the outside in order to screen those mounting up into the Upper Paradise that they should not be seen by those remaining below.

— *Zohar* 4:210b-211a, Sperling 4:216

After its judgment, the weighing in the balance of good against evil, the nĕshāmāh is purified in the River of Fire (*nĕhar dī-nūr*). The nĕshāmāh originated in fire and, hence, must be cleansed by fire alone, to purify it and separate away the earthly dross. It is plunged into the River of Fire which cleanses without consuming. Speaking of the ascent of the nĕshāmāh to the superior Paradise or Garden of Eden, the *Zohar* says:

A second ordeal has to be undergone by the soul on its passage from Lower Paradise to Upper Paradise; for whilst in Lower Paradise it is not yet entirely purged of the materialities of this world, so as to be fit to ascend on high. They thus pass it through that "river of fire" from which it emerges completely purified and so comes before the presence of the Sovereign of the universe beatified in every aspect. Also the rays of the celestial light afford it healing. This is its final stage. At that stage the souls stand garbed in their raiment and adorned in their crowns before their Master.

— 4:211b, Sperling 4:219-20

These abodes of the soul after death are among the ten firmaments spoken of in the *Zohar*. The seven manifested firmaments are associated with the various "earths," which are analogous to the globes of the earth planetary chain in theosophy.

> Between each earth and the next is a firmament which divides them from one another. Hence they all have separate names, among them being the Garden of Eden and Gehinnom. The creatures in them also are different, corresponding to those above, some with two faces, some with four, and some with one; and their aspects also differ. . . . This mystery [that there are seven earths enveloping one another] has been entrusted to the masters of wisdom, but is not known to those who mark out boundaries.
>
> — *Zohar* 4:10a, Sperling 4:346-7

Above the lower seven firmaments is a firmament of no color, beyond human comprehension, which diffuses light to all and

> speeds them each on its fitting orbit. Beyond that firmament knowledge cannot penetrate, and man must close his mouth and not seek to reflect upon it. He who does so reflect is turned backwards, for it passes our knowledge. . . . their mystery can be comprehended only by the wise of heart.
>
> — *Zohar* 4:164b, Sperling 4:68

It is said that the garments of the inferior Eden are made of our good actions, while the garments of the superior Eden are formed of the devotion and earnestness of our spirit. In the *Zohar* this is called devotion to the Tōrāh, which represents truth and the divine mysteries. The *Zohar* also says that the Tōrāh and compassion are in essence identical. Thus the importance of loving the Tōrāh, of having supreme devotion and dedication to the Law or truth. The written word is incidental and unimportant by itself. One's devotion is to the oral or esoteric Tōrāh, the spirit of truth and the fraternity of teachers who expound that oral or secret Sōd, the Mysteries.

> All the Companions in the time of R. Simeon loved one another with heart and soul, and therefore in his generation the secrets were revealed; for he was wont to say that students of the Holy Torah who do not love one another cause a departure from the right path, and what is even more serious, cause a blemish in the very Torah itself, for the Torah is the essence of love, brotherhood, and truth.
>
> — *Zohar* 4:190b, Sperling 4:142

The Tōrāh opens up communication between the soul and the superior worlds, sustaining all things, for with it the Holy One nourished the world: "whenever the Torah is studied by night, a little thread of this hidden light steals down and plays upon them that are absorbed in their study . . ." (*Zohar* 4:149a, Sperling 4:21). Those "who are importunate for any word of esoteric wisdom, who study it minutely and patiently to discover its true significance and so to gain knowledge of their Lord" are the ones who will enter the company of the angels "and pass through all the celestial gates without let or hindrance" (*Zohar* 2:130b, Sperling 2:20).

Knowledge of the Tōrāh is said to make the way smooth after death, as it makes known the paths of those realms and in fact guards the departed, not unlike the Tibetan "Book of the Dead." It leads the soul on its upward journey, standing by it "when he is awakened at the resurrection of the dead, in order to defend him against any accusations." Those who studied the Tōrāh will be more skillful after death than they were before, "so that points which formerly baffled them in spite of all their labour will now be fully comprehended by them, the Torah itself speaking within them" (*Zohar* 2:185a, Sperling 2:206).

> Now the tree of life ramifies into various degrees, all differing from one another, although forming a unity, in the shape of branches, leaves, bark, stock, and roots. All the faithful ones of Israel lay hold upon the tree of life, some grasping the stock, some the branches, some the leaves, and others, again, the roots. But those who exert themselves in the study of the Torah grasp the very trunk of the tree, and so lay hold upon all; and so we affirm.
>
> — *Zohar* 2:193a-b, Sperling 2:235-6

The *Bhagavad-Gītā* and other scriptures contain the same injunction: "he who is devoted to me, becomes at one with me (Krishna), is blessed, and receives the supreme spirit within him." This is devotion to truth, zeal for its study, loyalty to its spiritualizing ideals, and dedication of the self to its demands in order to become that truth itself — for the sharing of its benedictions with the world. All this transmutes the base within us into gold, spiritualizes the nefesh, raising it from animal to human, and from human to divinity. The precepts of the Tōrāh "fashion a glorious garment" for the spirit, and for the soul after death, and a glorious garment on earth, "and man requires them all" (*Zohar* 2:226b, Sperling 2:326).

Spiritual growth and initiation are among the running

themes in Qabbālāh. The assemblies or secret mysteries of the Hebrews were called Sōd, reminiscent of the Greek word *mystērion* (mystery). The word occurs frequently in the Old Testament, translated as "secret" or "assembly," where "Mysteries" would perhaps be more apt. In connection with Sōd was the Sodalian Oath of secrecy, the breaking of which meant "death" to the betrayer.

In explaining the hidden nature of the deeper wisdom, the *Zohar* says that the supernal primordial light which came forth when God said, "Let there be light," shone for one day and then was hidden away, although it continues to sustain all the worlds "by secret paths which cannot be discovered" (*Zohar* 1:30b, Sperling 1:116).

> There is a graduated series of the intimations by which deeper knowledge is conveyed to men, dreams forming one grade, vision another grade, and prophecy a third grade, in a rising series. — *Zohar* 2:183a, Sperling 2:199

Man was created with the faculty to perfect himself in the service of the Divine and to direct his life so that he would merit the hidden celestial light reserved for the righteous.

Initiation stories are found throughout the *Zohar*, which states that God sends tests to the righteous in order to glorify them. The Satan (adversary, opposer) of exoteric Judaism and Christianity is a product of theological imagination. Many biblical scholars point out that the Satan of the *Book of Job* was an angel sent by God to test the character of Job. The adverse forces of nature are the means by which each one of us tests our will and determination to grow in spirit, mind, and heart.

Moses ascended the mountain, spoke with God, and returned glorified, bringing the divine message to the Hebrew people. Probably all peoples have had a holy mountain, such as Meru, Parnassus, Olympus, or Aetna. All these represented "places of initiation and the abodes of the *chiefs* of the communities of ancient and even modern adepts" (*SD* 2:494).

A third example of initiation is the story of Jonah, swallowed by the great fish. Therein, protected, he saw "an open space like unto the halls of a palace, and the two eyes of the fish shining like the sun at noon. Inside was a precious stone which illumined all around, and made visible to him all the wonders of the deep" (*Zohar* 3:48a, Sperling 3:146). God, seeing his enjoyment, killed the fish, and other fishes ate "its carcase from all sides so that Jonah found himself in dire straits, and it was then that he prayed 'from out of the belly of sheol,' to wit, of the dead fish" — but also the underworld of the dead. "'And Jonah prayed unto the Lord *his* God out of the fish's belly'; i.e. to the grade of the Deity to which he was attached" (*Zohar* 3:48a, Sperling 3:146-7). God then brought the great fish back to life, and it rose up onto the land and vomited Jonah forth.

Sometimes the secret wisdom or knowledge is conceived of as a chariot (merkābāh) because esoteric wisdom is the vehicle for the communication to human consciousness of the mysteries of the universe and of man. God descends, using the form of the archetypal man as a vehicle or chariot for the expression of divinity below.

What advice does the *Zohar* give those who wish to progress spiritually? We have already discussed right thought and conduct, sincere repentance, love of truth, and study of the Tōrāh or Law. Self-control is recommended; anger, for instance, is called a form of idolatry, "since it actually sets up an idol in the very heart of him who is angered . . . because he has uprooted the holiness of his soul from its place and the 'other god' has entrenched himself therein, . . ."

> when a man uproots the holiness of his soul and is given admission to that "strange god" in its place — the "strange god" which is called "impure"— that man has become polluted and he pollutes everyone with whom he comes into contact, and holiness flees from him; . . .
>
> — *Zohar* 4:182b, Sperling 4:118

To achieve the spirit of holiness requires "strenuous effort, purification of one's self and one's dwelling, devotion of heart and soul; and even so one will be lucky to win it to take up its abode with him" (*Zohar* 3:128a, Sperling 3:364). Of great importance is the practice of concentration or prayer, which is "spiritual worship. Deep mysteries are attached to it, for men wot not that a man's prayer cleaves the ethereal spaces, cleaves the firmament, opens doors and ascends on high" (*Zohar* 4:201a, Sperling 4:181). This prayer is contemplation, not petitionary prayer. Such practice allows us to "see" with the closed eye.

> The closed eye sees the mirror of light: the open eye sees the mirror which is not luminous. Therefore in regard to the lightless mirror, the term "see" is used, because it is discernible, but in regard to the luminous mirror the term "know" is used, because it is in concealment.
>
> — *Zohar* 3:23b, Sperling 3:78

Sperling explains that "The idea seems to be that just as these [luminous colors] can only be seen when the eye is closed, so the higher emanations can only be grasped when the mind completely abstracts itself from the perceptions of sense" (*Zohar* 3:23b, Sperling 3:78n).

The seeker after the divine mysteries should concentrate the mind on the highest, while realizing that higher still is the unknowable, the concealed starting-point.

It is the desire of the upward-striving thought to pursue after this and to be illumined by it. In the process a certain fragment is detached, and from that fragment, through the pursuit of the upward-striving thought, which reaches and yet does not reach it, there is a certain illumination. The upward-striving thought is thus illumined by a light undisclosed and unknowable even to that thought. That unknowable light of Thought impinges on the light of the detached fragment which radiates from the unknowable and undisclosed, so that they are fused into one light, from which are formed nine Palaces. These Palaces are neither lights nor spirits nor souls, neither is there anyone who can grasp them. The longing of the nine illuminations which are all centred in the Thought — the latter being indeed counted as one of them — is to pursue these Palaces at the time when they are stationed in the thought, though they are not (even then) grasped or known, nor are they attained by the highest effort of the mind or the thought. All the mysteries of faith are contained in those Palaces, and all those lights which proceed from the mystic supreme Thought are called *EN-SOF* (Limitless). Up to this point the lights reach and yet do not reach: this is beyond the attainment of mind and thought. When Thought illumines, though from what source is not known, it is clothed and enveloped in *Binah* (understanding), and then further lights appear and one is embraced with the other until all are intertwined.

— *Zohar* 1:65a, Sperling 1:212-13

The *Zohar* says, "for none is a more interior abode reserved than for those who penetrate into the divine mystical doctrines and enter each day into close union with their Divine Master" (2:130b, Sperling 2:19). The final goal is unity of all the inner aspects with the divine.

> Happy is the portion of whoever can penetrate into the mysteries of his Master and become absorbed into Him, as it were. Especially does a man achieve this when he offers up his prayer to his Master in intense devotion, his will then becoming as the flame inseparable from the coal, and his mind concentrated on the unity of the lower firmaments, to unify them by means of a lower name, then on the unity of the higher firmaments, and finally on the absorption of them all into that most high firmament. Whilst a man's mouth and lips are moving, his heart and will must soar to the height of heights, so as to acknowledge the unity of the whole in virtue of the mystery of mysteries in which all ideas, all wills and all thoughts find their goal, to wit, the mystery of the *En-Sof* (Infinite, Illimitable).

> — *Zohar* 4:213b, Sperling 4:224-5

The mystical teachings of the Hebrews bear the insignia of the ancient wisdom-religion, paralleling the inner teachings of the other great world religions concerning the nature of the human being and the paths followed in sleep, death, and initiation. This unity of essence should not surprise us when we remember that all the great systems of thought and inquiry spring from an identic source: the brotherhood of spiritually advanced human beings and the inner core of each individual, which is identic with the core of every other being.

Hebrew Pronunciation Guide

Consonants:

ʾ	אָ אֲ	silent	אָדָם	ʾādām, "human being"
b	בַּ	**b** in bed	בִּינָה	Bīnāh, 3rd sĕfīrāh
	בְ	**v** in vine	גְּבוּרָה	Gĕbūrāh, 5th sĕfīrāh
g	גָּ	**g** in get	גָּבַר	gābar, "to be strong"
	גָ	**g** (guttural)	דָּג	dāg, "fish"
d	דָּ	**d** in doctor	דָּבָר	dābār, "word"
	ד	**th** in then	תַּלְמוּד	Talmūd
h	הַ	**h** in how	הוֹד	hōd, "splendor"
	הַ	an aspirate	גָּבָהּ	gābāh, "lofty"
v	ו	**v** in voice	יְהֹוָה	Yĕhovāh
w		**w** in water	וָו	wāw
z	זּ ז	**z** in zeal	זֹהַר	Zohar
ḥ	ח	**ch** in Loch Ness	חֶסֶד	Ḥesed, 4th sĕfīrāh
ṭ	ט ט	**t** in tie	טוֹב	ṭōb, "good"

y	י ֫	y in yodel	יָצַר	yātsar, "to form"
k	כ ךְ	k in kite	כֶּתֶר	Kether, 1st sĕfīrāh
kh	כ ך	kh in khaki	מַלְכוּת	Malkhūth, 10th sĕfīrāh
l	ל לְ	l in light	לוֹט	lōṭ, "veil"
m	ם מ מ	m in memory	מָיִם	māyim, "waters"
n	ן נ נ	n in narrow	נוֹחַ	Nōaḥ
s	ס ס	s in soft	סֵפֶר	sēfer, "book"
ʿ	ע	guttural sound	עוֹלָם	ʿōlām, "world"
p	פ	p in paper	פָּאַר	pāʾar, "to be beautiful"
f	ף פ	f in form	תִּפְאֶרֶת	Tifʾereth, 6th sĕfīrāh
ts	צ צ ץ	tz in Fritz	נֶצַח	Netsaḥ, 7th sĕfīrāh
q	ק ק	hard q (no u sound)	קַבָּלָה	Qabbālāh
r	ר רִ	r in roar	אוֹר	ʾōr, "light"
sh	שׁ שׁ	strong sh in shelf	שָׁלוֹם	shālōm, "peace"
ś	שׂ שׂ	soft sh	שָׂרָה	śārāh, "princess"
t	ט	t in tone	תַּנָּאִים	tannāʾīm, "teachers"
th	ת	th in theosophy	סְפִירוֹת	sĕfīrōth, "numbers"

Vowels

ā	ָ	**a** in father	דָּג	dāg, "fish"
a	ַ	**a** in calf	בַּת	bath, "daughter"
a	ֲ	**a** (almost silent)	רַחֲמִים	raḥamīm, "love"
e	ֶ	**e** in fellow	נֶפֶשׁ	nefesh
e	ֱ	**e** in met	אֱלֹהִים	'elohīm, "divine ones"
ē	ֵ	**ey** in they	שֵׁם	shēm, "name"
i	ִ	**i** in kilo	מִן	min, "from"
ī	יִ	**i** in machine	עוֹלָמִים	'ōlāmīm, "worlds"
o	ֹ	**o** in alone	תֹהוּ	tohū, "desolation"
ō	וֹ	**o** in both	הוֹד	Ḥōd, 8th sĕfīrāh
o	ָ	**au** in haul	חָכְמָה	Ḥokhmāh, 2nd sĕfīrāh
u	ֻ	**oo** in toot	סֻלָּם	sullām, "ladder"
ū	וּ	**oo** in boot	קוּם	qūm, "to arise"
ai	ַי	**i** in sigh	אֵל חַי	'ēl ḥai, "living being"
āi	ָי	**ei** in height	אֲדֹנָי	'adonāi, "my lords"
ēi	ֵי	**ai** in pain	בֵּית	bēith, "house"
ĕ	ְ	almost silent e	יְסוֹד	Yĕsōd, 9th sĕfīrāh
	ְ	closes a syllable	קַדְמוֹן	qadmōn, "ancient"

Glossary of Qabbalistic Terms

'āb, אָב, Father, title of the second sĕfīrāh, Ḥokhmāh.

'Ādām 'Illā'āh, אָדָם עִלָּאָה, Highest Adam: 'ādām, human being, masculine or feminine, its singular form being used collectively for humanity; 'illā'āh, עִלָּאָה, supernal, highest, from the verb 'ālāh, עָלָה, to ascend, to rise.

'Ādām Qadmōn, אָדָם קַדְמוֹן, Eastern or Ancient Adam: 'ādām, man or human being; qadmōn, קַדְמוֹן, eastern, ancient, foremost, from the verb qādam, קָדַם, to go before, to precede, to be ancient, with a secondary meaning to go towards the east. Hence 'Ādām Qadmōn is the archetypal human being.

'adonāi, אֲדֹנָי, my lords (not "Lord"); divine name of Malkhūth, the tenth sĕfīrāh.

'anpīn, אַנְפִּין (Aramaic), faces, (Hebrew pānīm, פָּנִים), plural form with both singular and plural significance.

'Arīkh 'Anpīn, אֲרִיךְ אַנְפִּין (Aramaic), long or extended face or countenance: 'arīkh, long, prolonged or extended, from the verb 'arakh, אֲרַךְ (Hebrew 'ārakh, אָרַךְ), to be long, to stretch, to expand, to endure; 'anpīn, plural, from an unused Aramaic singular 'anaf, אֲנַף, 'anpīn having both a singular and plural significance; cf. Zĕ'eir 'Anpīn.

'attīq yōmīn, עַתִּיק יוֹמִין (Aramaic), Ancient of Days: 'attīq, ancient; yōmīn, days (singular, yom, יוֹם).

'attīqā' dĕ'attīqīn, עַתִּיקָא דְעַתִּיקִין (Aramaic), The Ancient of the Ancient Ones, from the verb *'athaq*, עָתַק (Hebrew *'āthaq*, עָתַק), to be old.

'attīqā' dĕ-kol 'attīqīn, עַתִּיקָא דְכֹל עַתִּיקִין (Aramaic), variant of the above, the Ancient of *all* the Ancient Ones: *dĕ*, prefix; *kol*, all, every.

'attīqā' qaddīshā', עַתִּיקָא קַדִּישָׁא (Aramaic), the Holy Ancient One: *'attīqā'*, ancient; *qaddīshā'* (Hebrew *qādōsh*, קָדוֹשׁ), holy, sacred, revered. A phrase used often for Kether: "And therefore is the Most Holy Ancient One called AIN ['Ayin], the Negatively Existent; seeing that back from Him dependeth the AIN, the Negative Existence" (*'Idrā' Zūṭā'* 2:65; cf. Mathers, p. 266).

'attīqā' sābā' dĕsābīn, עַתִּיקָא סָבָא דְסָבִין (Aramaic), variant of the above, the Archaic Oldest of the Oldest or, according to Mathers, the "Eternal Ancient of the Ancients"— suggesting infinity, *'ēin sōf*; *'attīqā'*, ancient; and *sābā'*, oldest.

Bīnāh, בִּינָה, intelligence, insight, understanding, the third sĕfīrāh, from the verb *bīn*, בִּין, to perceive, to discern, to understand. Bīnāh is the feminine stream of passive energy flowing from Kether through Ḥokhmāh, forming the left shoulder of 'Ādām Qadmōn.

bohū, בֹּהוּ, chaotic condition; often used with tohū.

Būtsīnā' dĕQardīnūthā', בּוּצִינָא דְקַרְדִּינוּתָא (Aramaic), translated by Isaac Myer as "brilliant inner light": *būtsīnā'*, also found in the *Zohar* as *bōtsīnā'*, בּוֹצִינָא, candle, lamp, light, from the verb *būts*, בּוּץ, to burst forth, to shine.

dĕDīnā', דְדִינָא (Aramaic), *dĕ*, prefix; *Dīnā'* (Hebrew *dīn*, דִּין), right, judgment, decision.

děHesed, דְּחֶסֶד (Aramaic), *dě*, prefix; *Hesed*, compassion, mercy, the fourth sěfīrāh.

dimyōn, דְּמְיוֹן, form, likeness, from the verb *dāmāh*, דָּמָה, to resemble, to be like, to image.

dīn, דִּין, right, judgment, decision, from the verb *dūn*, דּוּן, to judge, to decide, to determine; an alternate name for the fifth sěfīrāh (Gěbūrāh, Paḥad).

dīqnā', דִּיקְנָא (Aramaic), beard, hair-growth.

dīqnā'di-měḥēiměnūthā', דִּיקְנָא דִּמְחֵימְנוּתָא (Aramaic), beard of truth: *dīqnā'*, beard; *di*, prefix; *měḥēiměnūthā'*, truth, confidence, faith, honor, from the verb *ḥēiman*, חֵימַן (Hebrew *'āman*, אָמַן), to have faith, to trust, to have confidence in.

diyyūqnā', דִּיוּקְנָא (Aramaic), image or likeness.

Dūmāh, דּוּמָה, Angel of Death.

'ehyeh, אֶהְיֶה, I am; divine name of Kether, the first sěfīrāh.

'ēinā' dě-'ashgāḥūthā', עֵינָא דְּאַשְׁגָּחוּתָא (Aramaic), eye of guardianship: *'ēinā'* (Hebrew *'ayin*, עַיִן), eye, sight, from the verb *'ūn*, עוּן, to watch, to guard, also to select, to meditate, to study and to speculate; *dě*, prefix; *'ashgāḥūthā'*, from *'ashgaḥ*, אַשְׁגַּח, from the verb *shěgaḥ*, שְׁגַח, to look, to care for, to guard (cf. Latin *providere*, to see forward, to discern, also to act with care, with foresight, hence Providence).

'ēinā' 'illā'āh, עֵינָא עִלָּאָה (Aramaic), supernal eye: *'ēinā'*, eye, see above; *'illā'āh*, supernal, highest, from *'ālāh*, עָלָה, to ascend, to rise.

'ēinā' pěqīḥā', עֵינָא פְּקִיחָא (Aramaic), open eye: *'ēinā'*, eye, see above; *pěqīḥā'*, from the verb *pěqaḥ*, פְּקַח (Hebrew *pāqaḥ*, פָּקַח), to open (the eye), also to guard, to care;

the open eye of Macroprosopus in contrast with both the closed eye of ʾein sōf, and the two eyes of Microprosopus that slumber and wake.

ʿeinā ʾqaddīshā ʾ, עֵינָא קַדִּישָׁא, holy eye: ʿeinā ʾ, eye, see above; qaddīshā ʾ, sacred, holy, revered.

ʾein sōf or sūf, אֵין סוֹף, no limit or end: ʾein, construct form of ʾayin, אַיִן, nothing, nought; sōf or sūf, limit, end, from the verb sūf, סוּף, to have an end; the Boundless (cf. Sanskrit parabrahman).

ʾēl, אֵל, the mighty one; divine name of Ḥesed, the fourth sĕfīrāh.

ʾēl ḥai, אֵל חַי, the mighty living being, the Lord of Life; divine name of Yesōd, the ninth sĕfīrāh.

ʾelōah or ʾelōha, אֱלוֹהַ, divine name of Gĕbūrāh, the fifth sĕfīrāh.

ʾelohīm, אֱלֹהִים, divine or mighty ones; divine name of Tifʾereth, the sixth sĕfīrāh.

ʾelohīm tsĕbāʾōth, אֱלֹהִים צְבָאוֹת, lord or lords of armies of beings; divine name of Hōd, the eighth sefīrāh.

ʾēm, אֵם, Mother (Aramaic ʾimmī, אִמִּי), name of Bīnāh.

ʿēts ḥayyīm, עֵץ חַיִּים, tree of lives; usually translated Tree of Life: ʿēts, tree; ḥayyīm, masculine plural noun from the verb ḥāyāh, חָיָה, to breathe, to blow, also to live; used in Qabbālāh for the tenfold sefīrōthal tree, the ten breaths or lives forming the complete tree or world. Also ʿēts ha ḥayyīm, עֵץ הַחַיִּים, (cf. Genesis 2:9).

galgillīm, גַּלְגִּלִּים, spheres, from the verb gālal, גָּלַל, to wheel, to turn, to revolve.

Gan ʿĒden, גַּן עֵדֶן, Garden of Eden.

gilgūlīm, גִּלְגּוּלִים (Aramaic *gilgūlā'*, גִּלְגּוּלָא), whirlings, with specific reference to the revolution of souls through a series of births and deaths; from the verb *gālal*, גָּלַל, to wheel, to turn, to revolve.

Gĕbūrāh, גְּבוּרָה, strength, power, might, from the verb *gābar*, גָּבַר, to be strong, mighty; the fifth sĕfīrāh, a feminine potency issuing from and complementing Ḥesed, its masculine counterpart; corresponding to the left arm of 'Ādām Qadmōn.

Gĕdūlāh, גְּדוּלָה, feminine noun, greatness, might, power, strength, from the verb *gādal*, גָּדַל, to grow, to become great, far-reaching in power; an alternate name for Ḥesed.

gūf, גּוּף, body, container of the life-breaths — nĕshāmāh, rūaḥ, and nefesh — that inform the human constitution.

gūlgaltā', גּוּלְגַּלְתָּא (Aramaic), skull, head, equivalent of Hebrew *gulgōleth*, גֻּלְגֹּלֶת, and Greek *golgotha*, γολγοθᾶ (*Matthew* 27:33), from the verb *gālal*, גָּלַל, to wheel, to turn, to revolve, with the extended meaning of something rolled or turned to hardness, i.e., the hardness of bone, a skull.

ḥai, חַי, vital principle in the human body.

Hā-'Idrā' Rabbā' Qaddīshā', הָאִדְרָא רַבָּא קַדִּישָׁא, The Great Holy Assembly, discourses of Shim'ōn ben Yoḥai to his disciples on the form of Deity and on pneumatology, science of *pneuma*, spirit.

Hā-'Idrā' Zūṭā' Qaddīshā', הָאִדְרָא זוּטָא קַדִּישָׁא, The Small Holy Assembly, discourses on the ten sĕfīrōth to six disciples.

ḥammāh, חַמָּה, warmth, light, from the verb *ḥāmam*, חָמַם, to be warm, to glow; name of the sun.

Ḥesed, חֶסֶד, ardor, zeal, love, goodness, compassion, mercy, from the verb *ḥāsad*, חָסַד, to be zealous towards, to feel kindness and love for, any person or thing; the fourth sĕfīrāh, a masculine active power, corresponding to the right arm of 'Ādām Qadmōn.

ḥiwyāi' bīshā', חִוְיָיא בִּישָׁא, evil beast.

Hōd, הוֹד, splendor, majesty; the eighth sĕfīrāh, a feminine potency representing the left thigh of 'Ādām Qadmōn.

Ḥokhmāh, חָכְמָה, skill, dexterity, hence wisdom, from the verb *ḥākham*, חָכַם, to be or become wise; the second sĕfīrāh, a right and masculine energy, termed the Duad or the Father, the right shoulder of 'Ādām Qadmōn.

ḥokhmĕthā' sĕthīmā'āh, חָכְמְתָא סְתִימָאָה, hidden wisdom: *ḥokhmĕthā'*, Aramaic form of Hebrew *ḥokhmāh*, חָכְמָה, signifying wisdom, learning, art, from the Aramaic verb *ḥakham*, חֲכַם (Hebrew *ḥākham*, חָכַם), to be wise, to be learned; *sĕthīmā'āh*, hidden, concealed, closed, from the Aramaic verb *sĕtham*, סְתַם (Hebrew *sātham*, סָתַם), to conceal, to hide, to shut.

ḥōṭāmā', חוֹטָמָא (Aramaic), the distinctive feature of the face, i.e., the nose, nostril, from the verb *ḥāṭam*, חָטַם, with a variety of meanings, among them to be prominent, to stand out, also to seal, to make an impression; cognate with root *ḥātham*, חָתַם, to seal, to enclose.

kēlīm, כֵּלִים, vessels, receptacles, from the verb *kālāh*, כָּלָה, to restrain.

Kether, כֶּתֶר, diadem, crown, from the verb *kāthar*, כָּתַר, to enclose, to surround; the first of the sĕfīrōth, called Sĕfī-rāh, the head or crown of the head of 'Ādām Qadmōn.

kether 'elyōn, כֶּתֶר עֶלְיוֹן, uppermost or highest crown: *kether*, crown, see above; *'elyōn*, from the verb *'ālāh*, עָלָה, to go up, to rise, to elevate.

kōkhāb, כּוֹכָב, name for Mercury; also a stellar body.

kūrsĕyā', כּוּרְסְיָא, throne.

lĕbānāh, לְבָנָה, white one, from the verb *lāban*, לָבַן, to grow white, to glisten, to be cleansed; a name for the moon.

ma'adīm, מַאֲדִים, fiery one, from the verb *'ādam*, אָדַם, to be red, fiery; a name of Mars.

mal'ākhayyā', מַלְאֲכַיָּא, messengers.

malkā', מַלְכָּא, Aramaic form of the Hebrew *melekh*.

malkā' qaddīshā', מַלְכָּא קַדִּישָׁא (Aramaic), holy or sacred king: *malkā'*, king; *qaddīshā'*, sacred, holy, revered.

malkhĕthā', מַלְכְּתָא (Aramaic), queen, from the Hebrew verb *mālakh*, מָלַךְ, to rule, to govern.

Malkhūth, מַלְכוּת, kingdom, dominion, from the verb *mālakh*, מָלַךְ, to reign, to be king; the tenth sĕfīrāh, the carrier or vehicle of the sefīrōthal powers, the feet of achetypal man; called also the Bride, Inferior Mother, or Queen.

māshīah, מָשִׁיחַ, anointed, i.e., initiated, from the verb *māshah*, מָשַׁח, to anoint; anglicized as Messiah.

mathqĕlā', מַתְקְלָא (Aramaic), weight, balance, from the verb *tĕqal*, תְּקַל (Hebrew *shāqal*, שָׁקַל), to weigh.

matrōnā', מַטְרוֹנָא (Aramaic), matron, lady, another name for the tenth sĕfīrāh, Malkhūth, the Queen, Bride of Tif'ereth (the King, Malkā' or Melekh).

maṭrōnīthā', מַטְרוֹנִיתָא (Aramaic), variant of *maṭrōnā'*, with identic meaning.

mazzālā' qaddīshā', מַזָּלָא קַדִּישָׁא (Aramaic), holy or sacred constellation, translated by Mathers as holy influence: *mazzālā'* (Hebrew *mazzāl*, מַזָּל), planet, constellation, luck, also fortune, destiny — by extension of thought, the influence from such planet or constellation, from the verb *nāzal*, נָזַל, to run, to flow, i.e., the influences that emanate from the planets and constellations; *qaddīshā'*, holy, revered, sacred.

mazzālōth, מַזָּלוֹת, constellations of the zodiac; plural of *mazzāl*, מַזָּל, a constellation, sometimes a planet, from the verb *nāzal*, נָזַל, to flow, to stream, to run*; the energies that flow or stream from the twelve zodiacal constellations through the planetary chains into the world. Also spelled *mazzārōth*, מַזָּרוֹת.

melekh, מֶלֶךְ, king, from the verb *mālakh*, מָלַךְ, to rule.

merkābāh, מֶרְכָּבָה, chariot.

Mĕṭaṭrōn, מְטַטְרוֹן, chief of the angels.

mishḥā', מְשִׁחָא (Aramaic), oil, marrow, fat, from the verb *māshaḥ*, מָשַׁח, to stroke over a thing, to anoint, to dedicate; cf. *māshīaḥ*.

mishḥā' di-rĕbūthā', מְשִׁחָא דִרְבוּתָא (Aramaic), oil of magnificence: *mishḥā'*, oil, see above; *di*, prefix; *rĕbūthā'*, greatness, dignity, office, anointment, from the verb *rĕbā'*, רְבָא (Hebrew *rābāh*, רָבָה), to grow, to increase, to become great.

---

*Cf. Greek verb *theō*, θέω, to run, anything circular; hence used for planets and the divinities (gods) of the planets.

mitsḥā', מִצְחָא (Aramaic form of Hebrew *mētsaḥ, מֵצַח*), the shining and high part, i.e., forehead, from the Hebrew verb *mātsaḥ, מָצַח*, to shine, to stand forth.

mōḥā', מוֹחָא (Aramaic), brain, head (Hebrew *mōaḥ, מוֹחַ*), with the original significance of marrow.

mōḥā' 'illā'āh, מוֹחָא עִלָּאָה, supernal brain: *mōḥā'*, brain, head, see above; *'illā'āh*, supernal, highest, from the verb *'ālāh, עָלָה*, to ascend, to go up; cf. *'Ādām 'Illā'āh*.

nefesh, נֶפֶשׁ, breath of life, from the verb nāfash, נָפַשׁ, to breathe; third of the three breaths that inform the human constitution; corresponds to the Greek *psuchē*, ψυχή.

nĕhar dī-nūr, נְהַר דִּינוּר, River of Fire.

nĕqūdāh pĕshūṭāh, נְקוּדָה פְּשׁוּטָה, expanded point: *nĕqūdāh*, point, dot, from the verb *nāqad, נָקַד*, to point, to puncture, to break through; *pĕshūṭāh*, from the verb *pāshaṭ, פָּשַׁט*, to stretch, to make plain, to extend, to unfold.

nĕqūdāh qadmā'āh, נְקוּדָה קַדְמָאָה, primordial or ancient point: *nĕqūdāh*, point, see above; *qadmā'āh*, primordial, ancient, preceding, also first, original.

nĕqūdāh ri'shōnāh, נְקוּדָה רִאשׁוֹנָה, first or original point: *nĕqūdāh*, point, see above; *ri'shōnāh*, first, original; Aramaic, *nĕqūdā' ri'shōnā', נְקוּדָא רִאשׁוֹנָא*.

nĕshāmāh, נְשָׁמָה, breath, spirit, wind, from the verb *nāsham, נָשַׁם*, to breathe, to blow; highest of the three breaths that inform the human constitution.

nĕshāmōth, נְשָׁמוֹת; plural of *nĕshāmāh*.

Netsaḥ, נֶצַח, glory, splendor, occasionally time, from the verb *nātsaḥ, נָצַח*, to shine, to be bright, to excel; the seventh *sĕfīrāh*, a masculine potency representing the right thigh in archetypal man.

nīmā', נִימָא (Aramaic), fringe, cord, hair, from the Hebrew verb *nāmāh*, נָמָה, to reach, to extend.

nogah, נֹגַהּ, brightness, light, from the verb *nāgah*, נָגַהּ, to be bright, to burst forth, to shine; name for Venus.

'ōfannīm, אוֹפַנִּים, wheels.

'ōlām, עוֹלָם, a period of time, hence a world or sphere, from the verb *'ālam*, עָלַם, to enwrap, to veil, to conceal, with a philosophical extension of meaning of hidden time, or an age or period whose birth and death are concealed from human knowledge.

'ōlām hā-'aśiyyāh, עוֹלָם הָעֲשִׂיָּה, world of action or construction: *'ōlām*, world, see above; *hā*, definite article; *'aśiyyāh*, from the verb *'āśāh*, עָשָׂה, to work, to labor, to form, to construct; the world of physical and material action or construction, the lowest of the four worlds.

'ōlām hā-'atstsīlōth, עוֹלָם הָאֲצִילוֹת, world of junction: *'ōlām*, world, see above; *hā*, definite article; *'atstsīlōth*, plural noun from the verb *'ātsal*, אָצַל, to join, to connect; the highest of the four worlds of Qabbālāh. Sometimes this world is given as *'ōlām has-sĕfīrōth*.

'ōlām hab-bĕrī'āh, עוֹלָם הַבְּרִיאָה, world of production or creation: *'ōlām*, world, see above; *hab*, definite article; *bĕrī'āh*, from the verb *bārā'*, בָּרָא, to form, to fashion, to produce, to shape, to carve; the sphere or world in which intellectual beings carve out future destiny to be unfolded in the lower *'ōlāmīm*; the next to the highest of the four worlds.

'ōlām haq-qĕlīppōth, עוֹלָם הַקְּלִיפוֹת, world of shells or rinds: *'ōlām*, world, see above; *haq*, definite article; *qĕlīppōth*, shells, rinds, skins.

ʿōlām has-sĕfîrōth, עוֹלָם הַסְפִירוֹת, world or sphere of emanation: *ʿōlām,* world, see above; *has,* definite article; *sĕfîrōth,* number, emanation; the highest world or sphere; cf. *ʿōlām hā-ʾatstsîlōth.*

ʿōlām hay-yĕtsîrāh, עוֹלָם הַיְצִירָה, world of formation: *ʿōlām,* world, see above; *hay,* definite article; *yĕtsîrāh* from the verb *yātsar,* יָצַר, to form, to fashion; the *ʿōlām* or world in which the forms as models are fashioned to be later condensed in the lowest *ʿōlām.*

ʿōlāmîm, עוֹלָמִים, worlds, spheres, planes, masculine plural of *ʿōlām.*

ʾōr, אוֹר, light, from the verb *ʾōr,* אוֹר, to break through, to shine, to enlighten; i.e., a breaking through from darkness (cf. *Genesis* 1:3, *yĕhî ʾōr,* יְהִי אוֹר, let there be light).

ʿōr, עוֹר, skin; also by extension, blindness, matter.

pahad, פַּחַד, fear, from the verb *pāhad,* פָּחַד, to fear, to be anxious.

partsûfîm, פַּרְצוּפִים, faces, used interchangeably with *partsûfîn* or *ʾanpîn.*

partsûfîn, פַּרְצוּפִין (Aramaic), plural noun adapted from the Greek *prosōpon,* πρόσωπον, face, visage.

Qabbālāh, קַבָּלָה, reception, tradition, from the verb *qābal,* קָבַל, or intensive active form *qibēl,* קִבֵּל, to receive, to admit a precept; hence the reception of the esoteric doctrine as it was orally transmitted.

qadmōn, see *ʾĀdām Qadmōn.*

qĕlîppōth, קְלִיפּוֹת, rinds, shells, parings, from the verb *qālaf,* קָלַף, to scrape, to peel, to pare. This word likewise signifies demons, entities in which spirit or light is recessive, and the husk or shell is dominant.

qĕrūmā' dĕ'awwēirā', קְרוּמָא דְּאַוֵּירָא (Aramaic), membrane or film of space: *qĕrūmā'*, skin, membrane, film, from verb *qĕram*, קְרַם (Hebrew *qāram*, קָרַם), to form a skin or film, to cover, to surround, to enclose; *dĕ'awwēirā'* (sometimes written *da'awēirā'*): *dĕ*, prefix; *'awwēirā'*, empty space, air, from the verb *'ōr*, אוֹר, to break through, to shine, to enlighten; (cf. Sanskrit *ākāśa*, the equivalent both etymologically and philosophically, from the verb *kāś*, to shine).

raḥamīm, רַחֲמִים, mercy, harmony, friendship, from the verb *rāḥam*, רָחַם, to have compassion, to be harmonious.

rātsōn, רָצוֹן, desire, goodwill, from the verb *rātsāh*, רָצָה, to be willing, to favor.

rēishā' ḥiwwārā', רֵישָׁא חִוָּרָא (Aramaic), white or bright head: *rēishā'* (Hebrew *ro'sh*, רֹאשׁ), head or chief; *ḥiwwārā'*, signifying clear, white, from the verb *ḥawar*, חֲוַר (Hebrew *ḥāwar*, חָוַר), to be white, to shine, to make clear; name for 'Arīkh 'Anpīn. Also written *Rĕ'sh Ḥiwwār*, רֵאשׁ חִוָּר.

rĕ'shīth hag-galgillīm, רֵאשִׁית הַגַּלְגִּלִּים, beginning of wheeling or turning: *rĕ'shīth*, first, beginning; *hag*, definite article; *galgillīm*, wheels, circlings, used of spheres or planets, from the verb *gālal*, גָּלַל (cf. *Sēfer Yĕtsīrāh* 2:4); the primum mobile, primordial motion; corresponding to Kether, the first sĕfīrāh.

rūaḥ, רוּחַ, wind, breath, spirit, from the verb *rūaḥ*, רוּחַ, to breathe, to blow; second of the three breaths that inform the human constitution.

rūḥīn, רוּחִין, plural of *rūaḥ*; also written *rūḥōth*, רוּחוֹת.

rūḥīn dĕHayyīn, רוּחִין דְּחַיִּין (Aramaic), spirits or breaths of lives: *rūḥīn*, plural of *rūaḥ*, רוּחַ, wind, breath, spirit; *dĕ*, prefix; *ḥayyīn*, plural of *ḥay*, חַי, the living.

sābā' dĕsābīn, סָבָא דְּסָבִין (Aramaic), the Oldest of the Oldest, from the verb *sĕ'ēb*, סָאֵב, or *sā'b*, סָאַב, meaning in its secondary form, to be old, to be hoary.

sālīq bi-rĕ'ūthā', סָלִיק בִּרְעוּתָא (Aramaic), highest in will or desire: *sālīq*, from the verb *sĕlēq*, סְלֵק, or *sĕlēiq*, סְלֵיק, to rise, to ascend; *bi*, prepositional prefix *bĕ*, בְּ, signifying "in" or "with"; *rĕ'ūthā'*, pleasure, will, from the verb *rĕ'ā'*, רְעָא, with secondary meaning to delight in, to desire; used for the Absolute, the supreme hierarch, i.e., the highest being who wills and desires the universe to flow forth from itself.

Sammā'ēl, סַמָּאֵל, Prince of Darkness or of Poison.

Sēfer Yĕtsīrāh, סֵפֶר יְצִירָה, "Book of Formation": *sēfer*, from the verb *sāfar*, סָפַר, to scratch, to engrave, hence to write, signifying a written treatise or book (in ancient times Hebrew books were generally written on rolls); *yĕtsīrāh*, from the verb *yātsar*, יָצַר, to form, to fashion; first of the great books of Qabbālāh, a work of cosmogonic character in which the 10 Numbers and 22 Letters form the 32 Paths of Wisdom. The same fundamental concept is found in the doctrine of Pythagoras that the universe was established in and on numbers.

Sĕfīrāh, סְפִירָה, feminine noun (plural *sĕfīrōth*, סְפִירוֹת), emanation, number; there is wide divergence of opinion among Hebrew scholars as to its exact definition, but the generally accepted derivation is from the verb *sāfar*, סָפַר, which in certain tenses may signify to count, to number. Hence, the term *sĕfīrāh* has come to imply the first number or emanation; and *sěfîrôth*, the succeeding numbers or emanations.

sěthīmā' dě-kol sěthīmīn, סְתִימָא דְּכֹל סְתִימִין (Aramaic), the Unknown of all the Unknown Ones, or the Hidden of all the Hidden Ones, from the verb *sětham*, סְתַם (Hebrew *sātham*, סָתַם), to close up, to keep secret, to keep unknown.

shabběthai, שַׁבְּתַי, from the verb *shābath*, שָׁבַת, to rest, to cease labor; the day of Sabbath, Saturn-day, preceding Sun-day.

shaddai, שַׁדַּי, the powerful, the mighty one; used of God only.

shěba' hêikhālōth, שֶׁבַע הֵיכָלֹות, the seven habitations.

shěkhīnāh, שְׁכִינָה (Aramaic *Shěkhīntā'*, שְׁכִינְתָּא), dwelling place, residence, from the verb *shākhan*, שָׁכַן (Aramaic *shěkhan*, שְׁכַן), to dwell, to rest.

shě'ōl, שְׁאֹול, the underworld, from the verb *shā'al*, שָׁאַל, to sink, to go down deep.

shib'āh kōkhābīm, שִׁבְעָה כֹּוכָבִים, seven luminous bodies: *shib'āh*, seven; *kōkhābīm*, stars or luminous bodies; in theosophical usage, the seven sacred planets.

Sifrā' di-Tsěnī'ūthā', סְפְרָא דִּצְנִיעוּתָא, Book of Concealment, discourses on cosmogony and demonology.

sithrā' děsithrīn, סִתְרָא דְּסִתְרִין (Aramaic), the Concealed of the Concealed Ones; from the verb *sěthar*, סְתַר (Hebrew *sāthar*, סָתַר), to hide, to conceal, to keep secret.

Sōd, סֹוד, council, assembly, also secret; in this latter sense used as the "secret mysteries" (cf. the Sodalian Oath, the breaking of which would cause "death" to the betrayer).

ṭallā', טַלָּא, Aramaic (Hebrew *ṭal*, טַל), dew, moisture, believed to drop from the heavens (shāmayim), from the verb *ṭĕlal*, טְלַל (Hebrew *ṭālal*, טָלַל), to hang over, to form drops, also to protect, to shelter.

Talmūd, תַּלְמוּד, instruction, discipline, from the verb *lāmad*, לָמַד, to beat with a rod, i.e., to discipline, to train, to teach.

ṭĕmīrā'diṭĕmīrīn, טְמִירָא דִטְמִירִין (Aramaic), the Hidden of the Hidden Ones, from the verb *ṭĕmar*, טְמַר, to hide, to preserve, to guard; also *ṭāmīr diṭĕmīrīn*, טָמִיר דִטְמִירִין.

Tif'ereth, תִּפְאֶרֶת, beauty, magnificence, glory, from the verb *pā'ar*, פָּאַר, to be beautiful, to glow; the sixth sĕfīrāh, representing the heart of 'Ādām Qadmōn and said to be the seat of the sun, from which flows into the surrounding and lower sĕfīrōth all goodness and inspiration. This sĕfīrāh is often termed the Small Countenance or Microprosopos, in contradistinction to Kether or Macroprosopos; *Tif'ereth* being inclusive of the six or nine sĕfīrōth which form Microprosopos in full.

tiqqūnīn, תִּקּוּנִין (Aramaic), plural of *tiqqūnā'*, תִּקּוּנָא, conformations, arrangements, orders, from the verb *tĕqēn*, תְּקֵן (Hebrew *tāqan*, תָּקַן), to be firm, to stand, to establish; refers specifically to the conformations or structures of 'Arīkh 'Anpīn and Zĕ'eir 'Anpīn. Also *tīqqūnā'*, תִּיקוּנָא, singular and *tīqqūnīn*, תִּיקוּנִין, plural.

tohū, תֹהוּ, waste, desolation, often used with bohū.

Tōrāh, תּוֹרָה, instruction, teaching, i.e., the Law, from the verb *yārāh*, יָרָה, signifying among other things to lay a foundation, hence to instruct, to teach. The Tōrāh comprises the first four books of the Pentateuch, some writers asserting that it stands for all five Mosaic books, and is written in Archaic or Biblical Hebrew.

tsedeq, צֶדֶק, victory, prosperity, power, from the verb tsādaq, צָדַק, to be strong, to be powerful, faithful, and true; a name of Jupiter.

tselā', צֵלָע, side, rib.

tselem, צֶלֶם, image, a likeness, from the verb tsālam, צָלַם, to shadow forth.

tsimtsūm, צִמְצוּם, contraction, restraint, from the verb tsā-mam, צָמַם, to press together, to restrain, to squeeze. Hence tsimtsūm is used in Qabbālāh to express the philosophic concept of contraction (and expansion).

tsūrāh, צוּרָה, prototype, from the verb tsūr, צוּר, to form, to fabricate.

yāh, יָה, divine name of Ḥokhmāh, the second sĕfīrāh.

Yĕhovāh, יְהוָה, divine name of Bīnāh, the third sĕfīrāh.

Yĕhovāh Tsĕbā'ōth, יְהוָה צְבָאוֹת, Lord of Hosts or Armies; divine name of Netsaḥ, the seventh sĕfīrāh.

yĕḥīdā'ḥad, יְחִידָא חַד (Aramaic), the one, the only: yĕḥīdā' (Hebrew yĕḥīdāh, יְחִידָה), from the verb yĕḥad, יְחַד (Hebrew yāḥad, יָחַד), to concentrate, to unite; ḥad, an abbreviated form of 'eḥād, אֶחָד, one.

Yĕsōd, יְסוֹד, foundation, from the verb yāsad, יָסַד, to set, to place, to lay a foundation; the ninth sĕfīrāh, representing the generative or productive power of 'Ādam Qadmōn.

yĕsōdōth, יְסוֹדוֹת, foundations or elements, from the verb yāsad, יָסַד, to lay a foundation, to establish, to support; corresponds to Malkhūth, the tenth sĕfīrāh, the foundation or carrier of all the sĕfīrōthic energies.

Zĕ'eir 'Anpīn, זְעֵיר אַנְפִּין (Aramaic), small or diminished face or countenance: *zĕ'eir,* small, young, reduced; *'anpīn,* face; cf. *'Arīkh 'Anpīn.*

zīqīn nītsōtsīn, זִיקִין נִיצוֹצִין (Aramaic), sparks of brilliance: *zīqīn,* sparks, plural noun from the verb *zānaq,* זָנַק, to eject with force, to shoot forth; *nītsōtsīn,* plural noun from the verb *nātsats,* נָצַץ, to sparkle, to blossom.

Zohar, זֹהַר, brightness, splendor, light in the sense of revelation, from the verb *zāhar,* זָהַר, to be bright, to shine, and in the causative sense to make light, hence to enlighten, to teach; the second of the great treatises of Qabbālāh.

Glossary of Theosophical Terms*

Ākāśa, (Sanskrit) "brilliant, shining, luminous," the fifth cosmic element, the "quintessence," called Aether by the ancient Stoics; the subtle, supersensuous spiritual essence which pervades all space.

Arūpa, (Skt) "formless," in the sense that the forms in the spiritual worlds are more ethereal than are those of the rūpa (form) worlds. In the septenary cosmos, the three higher planes are termed arūpa planes.

Ātma-buddhi, (Skt) the divine-spiritual part of a human being.

Ātman, (Skt) "self," the highest part of a human being: pure consciousness, that cosmic self which is the same in every human being. Ātman is the first principle in man; used also for the universal self or spirit.

Auric Egg, ranges from the divine to the astral-physical; the seat of all the monadic, spiritual, intellectual, mental, passional, and vital energies and faculties.

Buddhi, (Skt) "to enlighten, to perceive, to awaken," the faculty which manifests as understanding, discrimination, and intuition. Buddhi is the second principle in man and the garment or vehicle of ātman.

*Adapted from G. de Purucker's *Occult Glossary* and the *Encyclopedic Theosophical Glossary* (www.theosociety.org/pasadena/etgloss/etg-hp.htm).

Buddhi-manas, (Skt) the higher ego, the principle of essential self-consciousness, especially when considered as enlightened by ātman.

Chāyā, (*Cchāyā*, Skt) "shadow, copy," the astral body or image of a person.

Dhyān-Chohans, (Skt-Tibetan) "lords of meditation," cosmic or planetary spirits. As the summit of the Hierarchy of Light, they imbody the ideation of the cosmic Logos. Man in his higher nature is an embryo dhyān-chohan.

Kāma, (Skt) "desire," the fourth principle in man, the impelling force in the human constitution; colorless, neither good nor bad, and becomes such only as the mind and soul direct its use. It is the seat of impulses, desires, and aspirations, considered in their energic aspect.

Kāma-rūpa, (Skt) "desire body," the part of man's inner constitution in which dwell desires, affections, hates, loves — the various mental and psychical energies.

Laya-center, (Skt) "dissolution," a point of disappearance, a zero-point; any point in space which becomes the center of active life, first on a higher plane and later descending into manifestation through and by the laya-centers of the lower planes; also any point where substance rebecomes homogeneous.

Loka(s), (Skt) "place, locality," more frequently a "world, sphere, or plane." There are rūpa-lokas and arūpa-lokas. Lokas are inseparable from *talas* as the two poles of a magnet.

Mahat, (Skt) "great," cosmic mind or intelligence, the fundamental cause of the intelligent operations of nature seen as an organism; the cosmic noumenon of matter.

Manas, (Skt) "to think, to cogitate, to reflect," the center of the ego-consciousness in man. When imbodied manas is dual, gravitating in its higher aspects toward buddhi and in its lower aspects toward kāma. The first is intuitive mind, the second the animal, ratiocinative consciousness, the lower mentality and passions of the personality. Manas is the third principle in man.

Mānasaputras, (Skt) from *manas*, "mind," and *putra*, "son," "sons of mind." *Mānasa*, "belonging to the mind or spirit" indicates beings who are endowed with the fire of self-consciousness which enables them to carry on trains of self-conscious thought and meditation. Hence the mānasaputras are children of cosmic mind, a race of dhyān-chohans particularly evolved along the lines of the mānasic principle. The mānasaputras are a mystery in the human constitution: they are both ourselves and a descent into us of our higher selves. They are entities from the buddhic hierarchy of compassion, from the luminous arc of evolving nature.

Māyā, (Skt) from *mā*, "to measure," and by extension of meaning "to effect, to form, to limit," translated as "illusion," however, not meaning that things do not exist, but that we are blinded and our mind colored by our own thoughts, and do not as yet arrive at the real interpretation and meaning of the world around us. "Maya or illusion is an element which enters into all finite things, for everything that exists has only a relative, not an absolute, reality, since the appearance which the hidden noumenon assumes for any observer depends upon his power of cognition" (*SD* 1:39).

Māyāvi-rūpa, (Skt) from *māyāvi,* "illusory," and *rūpa,* "form," a "thought-body" or "illusory-body," a higher astral-mental form.

Monad, "individual, atom," from the Greek *monas,* "one, unit." A spiritual entity which, to human awareness, is indivisible; a divine-spiritual life-atom in contrast to that of the physical atom which is divisible, a composite heterogeneous particle. Monads are eternal, unitary, individual life-centers, conscious-ness-centers, self-motivated, self-conscious, in infinitely varying degrees, the ultimate elements of the universe.

Mūlaprakṛiti, (Skt) from *mūla,* "root," and *prakṛiti,* "nature," root-matter or root-nature; undifferentiated cosmic substance in its highest form, the abstract substance or essence of what later through various differentiations become the prakṛitis, the various forms of matter.

Parabrahman, (Skt) from *para,* "beyond," and *Brahman,* "universal self or spirit," that which is beyond Brahman; the self-enduring, eternal, self-sufficient cause of all, the one essence of everything in the cosmos.

Paramātman, (Skt) from *para,* "beyond," and *ātman,* "self," the "primordial self" or the "self beyond," the universal spirit-soul. Paramātman consequently means the "supreme self," or the summit or flower of a hierarchy, the root-base or source of that cosmic self.

Planetary Chain. Every cosmic body or globe, be it sun or planet, nebula or comet, atom or electron, is a composite entity comprised of inner and invisible energies and substances, and of an outer and often visible physical body. These elements all together are the principles or elements of every self-contained entity or individual life-center. A planetary chain is an entity composed of seven, ten, or twelve such multiprincipled globes, and which taken as a unit, forms one planetary chain. All celestial bodies are multiprincipled entities as man is, who is a copy in the small of what the universe is in the great.

Prajāpati, (Skt) from *pra*, "forth," *jan*, "to be born," and "*pati*, "lord," lord or master of progeny. Brahmā as Prajāpati symbolizes the collective creators of the universe with all its numberless hierarchical productions of things movable and seemingly immovable.

Prāṇa, (Skt) from *pra*, "before," and *an*, "to breathe, to blow, to live," usually translated "life," but rather the psycho-electrical field manifesting in the individual as vitality, commonly called "life principle." Prāṇa is the fifth principle in man.

Root-races. During evolution on our earth, mankind as a life-wave passes through seven evolutionary stages called Root-races. Each such Root-race contains many and various races as the word is commonly understood. All human beings alive today are part of the fifth Root-race.

Rūpa, (Skt) "form, image," signifies an atomic or monadic aggregation about the central and indwelling consciousness, forming a vehicle or body thereof, and is contrasted with arūpa (formless).

Sthūla-śarīra, (Skt) *sthūla*, "coarse, gross," bulky, differentiated matter, *śarīra*, "form"; the physical body, the seventh principle in man.

Svabhavat, (Skt) from *sva*, "self," and *bhū*, "to become, to be," that which becomes itself, which develops from within outwardly its essential self by emanation or evolution.

Tala(s), (Skt) "inferior world," used both in contrast to and in conjunction with *loka* (place, world), stands for the material aspects or substance-principles, in contrast to the lokas which denote the spiritual aspects of the universe.

Zoharic Writings

Hā-'Idrā' Rabbā' Qaddīshā', הָאִדְרָא רַבָּא קַדִּישָׁא, "The Great Holy Assembly," discourses of Shim'ōn ben Yoḥai to his disciples on the form of Deity and on pneumatology, science of *pneuma*, spirit.

Hā-'Idrā' Zūṭā' Qaddīshā', הָאִדְרָא זוּטָא קַדִּישָׁא, "The Small Holy Assembly," discourses on the sĕfīrōth to six disciples.

Hēikhālōth, הֵיכָלוֹת, "Mansions or Abodes," usually enumerated as seven, describing the structure of the upper and lower realms.

Midrāsh Han-Ne'ĕlām, מִדְרָשׁ הַנֶּעְלָם, "The Hidden Interpretation," deducing esoteric doctrine from the narratives in the Pentateuch.

Ra'yā' Mĕhēimnā', רַעְיָא מְהֵימְנָא, "The Faithful Shepherd," recording discussions between Moses the faithful shepherd, the prophet Elijah, and Rabbi Shim'ōn ben Yoḥai.

Rāzeī dĕ Rāzīn, רָזֵידְרָזִין, "Secrets of Secrets," a treatise on physiognomy and higher psychology.

Sābā' dĕ Mishpāṭīm, סָבָא דְמִשְׁפָּטִים, "The Aged in Decisions, Judgments"; the Aged One or Scholar is Elijah who discourses with Shim'ōn ben Yoḥai on the doctrine of metempsychosis.

Sifrā' di-Tsĕnī'ūthā', סִפְרָא דִצְנִיעוּתָא, "Book of Conceal-ment," discourses on cosmogony and demonology.

Sithrēi Tōrāh, סִתְרֵי תּוֹרָה, "Mysteries or Secrets of the Law," describing the evolution of the sĕfīrōth.

Tōseftā', תּוֹסֶפְתָּא, "Additions or Supplements."

Yānūqā', יָנוּקָא, *Yĕnōqā'*, יְנוֹקָא, "The Youth," discourses on the mysteries of ablutions by a young man of such high talent he was thought to be of superhuman origin.

Sources

Barker, A. Trevor, comp., *The Mahatma Letters to A. P. Sinnett*, 2nd ed. (1926), Theosophical University Press (TUP), Pasadena, 1992.

Blavatsky, H. P.:
Collected Writings, Vol. VII, 2nd ed., The Theosophical Publishing House, Wheaton, 1975.
Isis Unveiled (1877), TUP, 1998.
The Secret Doctrine (1888), TUP, 1999.
The Theosophical Glossary (1892), The Theosophy Company, Los Angeles, 1990.

Cohen, The Rev. Dr. A., *Everyman's Talmud*, J. M. Dent & Sons, Ltd., London, 1943; reprint Schocken Books, Inc., New York, 1995.

Franck, Adolph, *The Kabbalah or the Religious Philosophy of the Hebrews* (1843), The Kabbalah Publishing Company, New York, 1926.

Ginsburg, Christian D., *The Kabbalah: Its Doctrines, Development and Literature* (1863), George Routledge & Sons, London, 1920; also in *The Essenes: Their History and Doctrines; The Kabbalah: Its Doctrines, Development and Literature,* The Macmillan Company, New York, 1956.

Grondal, Florence Armstrong, *The Romance of Astronomy: The Music of the Spheres,* The Macmillan Company, New York, 1937.

Hanson Ph.D., Kenneth, *Kabbalah: Three Thousand Years of Mystic Tradition,* Council Oak Books, Tulsa, 1998.

Idel, Moshe, *Kabbalah: New Perspectives,* Yale University Press, New Haven and London, 1988.

Judge, William Q., *Bhagavad-Gita* (1890) *combined with Essays on the Gita* (1887-96), TUP, 1978.

Mathers, S. L. MacGregor, *The Kabbalah Unveiled*, George Redway, London, 1887; reprint Samuel Weiser, Inc., York Beach, ME, 1992.

Matt, Daniel C., *The Zohar, Pritzker Edition*, vol. 1, Stanford University Press, Stanford, 2004.

Myer, Isaac, *Qabbalah* (1888), Samuel Weiser, Inc., New York, 1974; also Wizards Bookshelf, San Diego, 1988.

Purucker, G. de:
   The Esoteric Tradition, 2nd ed. (1940), TUP, 1973.
   Fountain-Source of Occultism, TUP, 1974.
   Fundamentals of the Esoteric Philosophy, TUP, 1979.

Radhakrishnan, S., *The Bhagavadgītā*, Harper & Row, New York, 1973.

Scholem, Gershom G.:
   On the Kabbalah and Its Symbolism, Schocken Books, New York, 1965.
   Major Trends in Jewish Mysticism, Schocken Publishing House, Jerusalem, 1941; reprint Schocken Books, New York, 1995.

Sperling, Harry, Maurice Simon, and Dr. Paul P. Levertoff, trans., *The Zohar*, The Soncino Press, London and Bournemouth, 1949.

Titchenell, Elsa-Brita, *The Masks of Odin*, TUP, 1985.

Wägner, Dr. W., *Asgard and the Gods*, W. Swan Sonnenschein & Allen, London, 1880.

Yates, Frances A., *The Occult Philosophy in the Elizabethan Age*, Routledge & Kegan Paul, Ltd., London, 1979.

Index